ALDERNEY
FORTRESS ISLAND

The Germans in Alderney, 1940–1945

T.X.H. PANTCHEFF

T0352643

First published 1981 by Phillimore & Co. Ltd.

Reprinted 1997, 2003, 2005, 2015, 2019

The History Press
97 St George's Place, Cheltenham,
Gloucestershire, GL50 3QB
www.thehistorypress.co.uk

British Library Cataloguing in Publication Data.
A catalogue record for this book is available from the British Library.

ISBN 978 0 7509 6492 0

Printed in Great Britain by TJ International Ltd, Padstow, Cornwall

Contents

Maps and Diagrams

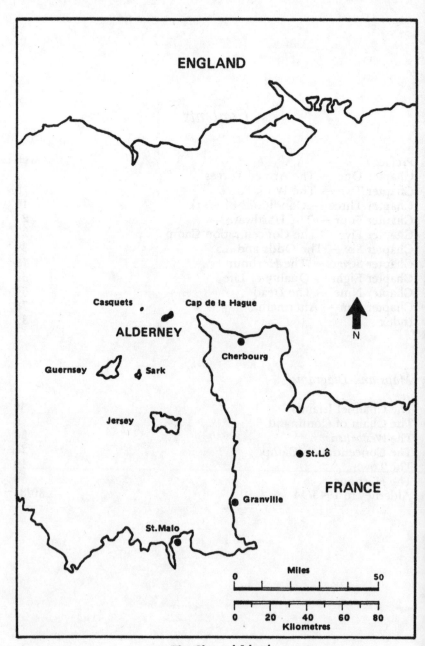

The Channel Islands

List of plates

Between pages 54 and 55

The author wishes to acknowledge:
Bundesarchiv, Federal Republic of Germany, for plates 1–3, 6, 8, 12, 18, 20, 22, 23, 25
Alderney Museum for plates 7, 10, 11, 13, 14, 16, 19, 21, 24, 28, 30–33
Alderney Picture Agency for plates 17, 26, 27
O. Johns for plate 15
J. Possnicker for plate 4
J.H. Wallbridge of Guernsey for plates 5, 9, 29

This book is dedicated to all those, of whatever
nationality, who died in Alderney or because
of events there during the Island's occupation
in the Second World War and who are therefore
unable to speak for themselves.

Acknowledgements

Thanks are due to all those who have helped with knowledge or advice; to those whose specialist expertise may, I hope, have got my terminology right; to those who have kindly read all or part of the text with a constructively critical eye. All errors and omissions are, of course, mine.

Particular thanks are due to Mr Colin Partridge for additional material on the hardware, for access to additional photographs from the Bundesarchiv, West Germany, and for much other data and assistance; to the Clerk to the States of Alderney for making their records available; to the Alderney Society and Museum in general and to Mr & Mrs K. Wilson in particular for the many photographs they put at my disposal and beyond that for kindness and encouragement; to Mr Owen Johns, Mr J. Possnicker and the Alderney Picture Agency for photographs.

Finally, my especial thanks first to those in the War Office in 1945 who sent me back to Alderney and thus made this book possible; and to my former secretary who volunteered to type my manuscript so that others might also be able to read it.

Preface

Alderney is one of the smaller islands in the group known as the Channel Islands, which retained their link to the English crown when the rest of the Duchy of Normandy was annexed by France in 1204. It is 3½ miles long and 1½ miles broad at its widest point. It lies 8 miles west of Cap de la Hague in mainland Normandy and 70 miles south–south–west of the Isle of Wight.

After overrunning northern France in early summer 1940, the German Armed Forces occupied the Channel Islands. What we are here concerned with, then, is what happened between the occupation of Alderney in July 1940 and its liberation by British Forces after the German capitulation in May 1945.

The history of Alderney during the years of the Second World War presents some unique difficulties. Until the evacuation of the Island by virtually the entire population in June 1940, events are fairly clear and documented and insofar as this may not be adequate there have been, and still are, witnesses enough to supplement or correct the record if they found fault. But after June 1940 the native witnesses were few indeed and far removed from the main stream of events in the Island. Contemporary or near-contemporary documentation of the German occupation of Alderney has inevitably been less detailed and satisfying than in the case of the other Channel Islands where a normal population experienced, recorded and remembered events and were able to cross-check what others might later say.

In the general absence of daily insight into life in Alderney between 1940 and 1945, some of the ground has been already covered with the help of such material as was available. In his definitive work 'The German Occupation of the Channel Islands' Dr. Charles Cruickshank has extracted from German, British and Channel Island official records a thorough survey of the historical issues governing German policy, its application in and its effect on all the islands, and he has fitted Alderney into this perspective as much as is warranted in a work of such breadth; it is inevitably not too concerned with the minutiae of Alderney, but I am indebted to him for much of the backcloth against which more detailed events will now be portrayed. Mr. Colin Partridge has approached the same rather 'empty quarter' from the field in which the most solid remaining evidence lies; in his 'Hitler's Atlantic

Wall' the major fortification works built by the Germans on Alderney are well treated, again in wider perspective. Colonel Packe and Mr. Dreyfus, in their 'Alderney Story', perhaps got nearest to the feel of the Island in the years of occupation, with the help of a variety of fragmentary sources (including a small contribution from myself). It is now the purpose of this book to amplify that fragment more fully, to put flesh on the concrete skeleton and to try to breathe life into it. We only go as far as the immediate aftermath in May 1945. After that date, the Islanders' return and the re-establishment of their own administration are another story; many were there who can tell it better than I.

On Alderney, few shots were fired in anger in the course of the War, except where casual air or sea targets of opportunity presented themselves. What, then, it may well be asked, happened in this tiny island that merits special mention? Two elements go to make up the answer to that question. First, Alderney was unique in being the only one of the British Isles under German occupation without a normal, resident civilian population. Secondly, Alderney has a human story to tell that has as yet only been told incompletely, piecemeal and sometimes with distortion. What did the grandiose German decrees actually mean on the ground to those who carried them out? What was the human price paid for all those wonder-works of concrete engineering? It matters to consider in more detail *what* happened, and *how*, in order to understand *why*.

By the close of the European war, scraps of information had already reached London suggesting that there had been some German malpractice on Alderney, so the War Office ordered an inquiry as soon as the islands were reoccupied by British Forces. I was charged with a substantial part of this inquiry on a brief from the Judge-Advocate General and spent most of May and June 1945 screening those Germans who had served in Alderney (some 3,000 of whom were immediately available as prisoners of war); questioning civilians who had relevant knowledge, particularly such former inmates of the forced labour camps as were still to hand; and instituting a search for material witnesses who had drifted further afield. Out of the interviews and interrogations in the course of this inquiry, a detailed picture emerged which, I feel, may now throw some new and useful light on the Island in those occupation years.

There have been a number of piecemeal accounts since those days. Some were the individual stories of a man's suffering, limited to his own knowledge but no less poignant for that. Some were the 'ear-witness' accounts of those who had seen little or nothing but had been told something. Some were recounted many years later—and occasionally had improved a bit in the telling, as comparison with what the same witness had said in 1945 could sometimes show. This book is based on the accounts of over 3,000 witnesses in 1945. Every German soldier in the Alderney garrison who was still to hand was seen. Every liberated prisoner or forced labourer from Alderney who was readily available was seen. This led to hundreds of written statements recorded at that time and from all these items of evidence, checked against each other and other sources, this account has ultimately been distilled. Of course it is not comprehensive: somebody somewhere may well know of an incident that has not yet come to light and it will be for them to build on the foundation here laid. But if the general picture can be presented on authentic evidence and in proper proportion this book will have served its purpose. If it does nothing else, at least it may help to lay some of the more fantastic ghosts so far raised—for example, the stories of gas-ovens in the concentration camp or bodies thrown into the cement-mixer (the venue varies with the version of the rumour).

This will disappoint the ghoulish who know of more inhuman practices under the Third Reich (or indeed elsewhere). It will also offend those who belive we should not rake over these ashes any more now that the Germans—at any rate the Federal Germans—are our friends, partners in the European Economic Community and allies in the North Atlantic Treaty Organisation. I would like to make my own position clear on these scores. I believe there is merit in putting any extended understanding of an historical truth on permanent record, be it good or bad.

But as we remember that Germans—officers, other ranks and non-combatants—did these things to fellow human beings, let us not forget that other Germans—also officers, other ranks and non-combatants—were as shocked by man's inhumanity to man as we ought to be. And these latter have been responsible for contributing in 1945 much of the testimony in this book.

T.X.H.P.

Alderney
1978–1981

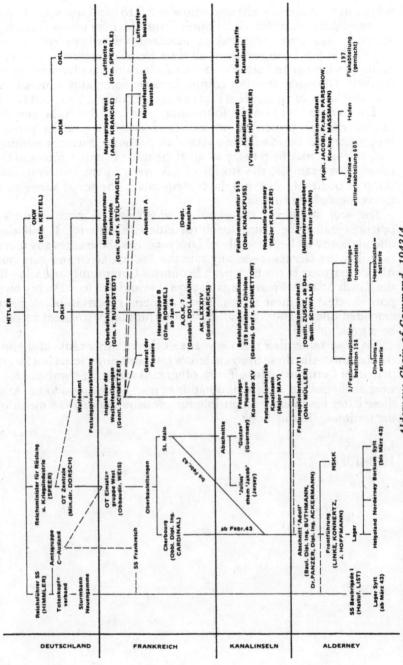

Alderney: Chain of Command, 1943/4

CHAPTER ONE

The Armed Forces

THE HIERARCHIC STRUCTURE of German military, para-military and ancillary forces in the Third Reich was perhaps rather more complex than that to which we may (or may even not) have been accustomed. If the reader is already conversant with that structure he will find much of this chapter a waste of time and is advised to skip fairly quickly to Chapter Two. If he or she is not so conversant it may regrettably be necessary to digest some homework now if there is to be understanding later of the events described and of the reasons why they happened in the way they did.

The *Organisation Todt* and the *Schutzstaffel* are explained in their appropriate place, Chapters Two and Five respectively. It is our purpose now to set the scene by considering the German Armed Forces of occupation.

The German Armed Forces (*Wehrmacht*) had a central, unified High Command (*Oberkommando der Wehrmacht* — OKW). Under OKW there was an individual High Command for each service: the Army (*Oberkommando des Heeres* — OKH), the Navy (*Oberkommando der Kriegsmarine* — OKM) and the Air Force (*Oberkommando der Luftwaffe* — OKL).

Although the majority of the garrison in Alderney for most of the occupation were soldiers and therefore subordinate to OKH, the general responsibility for coastal artillery rested with the Navy, subordinate to OKM, and the general responsibility for anti-aircraft defence lay with the Air Force, subordinate to OKL; each of these constituted a substantial minority on Alderney. To complicate things further there were exceptions, and the Army also manned some coastal and anti-aircraft guns of its own. In the small compass of Alderney all were represented, cheek by jowl with one another. The channels for discipline, command and sometimes supply were different and a potential source of friction, whatever attempts were made to rationalise the position on the ground.

In the occupied Channel Islands, army personnel fell into two broad categories: the field army, which had just conquered France, and the administrators. The garrisons as such were part of the field army and initially subordinated to the Corps, Army and Army Group headquarters in Occupied France. From 1941 the formation supplying these garrisons was 319 Infantry Division, which retained its identity right to the end of the war although the concept of a field force gave way to a fortress role from the end of 1941 onwards.

The Military Government element in the Islands was *Feldkommandantur* (FK) 515, centred in Jersey. It was part of the Military Government structure administering occupied France, responsible to the Military Governor in Paris and ultimately to OKH. It is interesting to note that if friction occurred between field army and administration, the nearest common authority by which both could be jointly commanded to comply if common sense did not prevail was OKH in Berlin. The *Feldkommandantur* was the administrative link between the occupying forces and the civil authorities which it supervised. FK 515 was represented in Alderney by an Out-Station (*Aussenstelle*). Because of the general absence of civil population and total absence of civil authorities, its role in practice tended to concentrate on managing property, agricultural activities and its own direct administrative functions, described in due course.

*   *   *

The first German troops landed in Alderney on 2 July 1940. The occupation which followed until May 1945 falls into two distinct periods, with the second of which this book is primarily concerned.

The early period covers the first year plus, that is the rest of 1940 and most of 1941. It must be remembered that in 1940 most Germans thought they had virtually won the war. Invasion of Britain, the only unconquered enemy in the field at that time, seemed imminent. The Channel Islands might be a useful part of the springboard for such a final operation, but did not immediately have any greater military significance.

The plan for occupation, which was a naval (OKM) responsibility, initially envisaged a total of six infantry battalions for the Islands, of which one was to occupy Alderney. In the event, token elements totalling only some eighty men landed in Alderney. They were commanded by a Sergeant who was formally designated Island Commandant (*Inselkommandant*) — first, briefly Schmidt, then Koch, followed by a series of NCOs and junior officers from 83 Infantry Division, a part of X Corps whose area embraced the neighbouring part of the French mainland. For unlike the other islands, which were controlled by 216 Infantry Division, also of X Corps, Alderney was until the beginning of 1942 run from Cherbourg.

Similarly, when the Out-Station of FK 515 arrived in Alderney it was organisationally part of the administration of the neighbouring French *département* (Manche) as far as the Germans were concerned. In the absence of a civil population to administer, one of their first tasks in this initial period was to develop the agricultural potential of Alderney to grow food for consumption in Guernsey. A working party from Guernsey began to give effect to this plan in Spring 1941.

By this time the German conception of the role of the Channel Islands was beginning to change. Hitler had already decided that when he had won the war there would be no question of handing the Islands back to the British Crown. They were to remain in perpetuity under German rule. The early plan considered detaching Alderney from the other islands and joining it to France after the war, but this intention does not seem to be reflected in the level of permanent concrete defence works which were developed on at least as dense a scale (for its size) as in Guernsey or Jersey. The Germans even dubbed Alderney 'The Gibraltar of the Channel'. The prestige factor in relation to Britain is here as apparent as the strategic factor in relation to a France that would no longer be occupied after the war. For the time being, Hitler was sensitive to the need to defend the Islands against coastal raids, which British Commandos had already started, or indeed against any attempt by British Forces to repossess them. The decisions to build large scale and permanent defence works in the Islands were therefore taken in steps through the summer and autumn of 1941, some months ahead of the decisions to build the Atlantic Wall to defend continental Europe from Norway to Spain.

The activities of FK 515's Out-Station reflected this change of attitude. In Spring 1941, under *Sonderführer** Herzog, they were supervising working parties to maintain the breakwater at Braye Harbour and to bring more land under cultivation. But these were followed by further working parties to recondition houses that were in some state of dilapidation, in anticipation of the increased garrison called for by Hitler's policy, and to build an extension to the existing harbour jetty to enable heavy barges to unload the stores required in quantity for the proposed defence works.

In October 1941, Hitler issued his Directive on the Fortification and Defence of the Channel Islands. This made OKH responsible for immediate and intensive work on strong concrete fortifications, envisaged a material stepping up in numbers and armament of the garrisons, and ordered the use of foreign labour to do the construction work, 'especially Russian and Spanish, but also French'. The occupation force in the Islands as a whole had been raised to divisional strength and placed under the command of 319 Infantry Division at the beginning of July 1941. 319 Infantry Division was a normal field

---

* The various grades of *Sonderführer*, for which there is no direct British equivalent, were a device to enable rank to be held by those whose service was necessary to the *Wehrmacht* but who were not properly serving members of the regular Armed Forces, for example, interpreters.

formation responsible through normal military hierarchical channels to LXXXIV Corps in St. Lô and thence to 7th Army HQ and so ultimately to the Commander-in-Chief West in Paris. The divisional commander of 319 Infantry Division was also designated overall Commander Channel Islands, with his overall Command HQ in Jersey and his Division HQ in Guernsey. Alderney itself, however, continued to be controlled by 83 Infantry Division until December 1941, when it, too, was placed under command of 319 Infantry Division.

In June 1941, the garrison in Alderney was about 450 strong. At the end of July the re-inforced 5th Company of 277 Grenadier Regiment arrived under a *Hauptmann* (Captain) Carl Hoffmann, who took over as Island Commandant. He established his headquarters in what is now the Connaught Hotel. By November 1941 there were nearly 2,500 Germans on Alderney — over 1,100 Army, some 200 Navy and 1,100 Air Force. These numbers were shortly to pass the 3,000 mark and the first labour contingent was about to arrive.

It is some measure of the increased responsibility under Hitler's new dispensation that the post of Island Commandant was taken from Hoffmann and given to a lieutenant-colonel (Gleden) by the end of the year. In the German Army at this time a battalion was normally commanded by a major, or even a senior captain. Hoffmann was a senior captain, and indeed promoted major before he left the Island in 1943 to command the III Battalion of 582 Grenadier Regiment in Jersey.

Gleden's few weeks as Island Commandant marked the end of the period when Alderney was under control of 83 Infantry Division. In January 1942, the new Island Commandant was briefly *Oberstleutnant* (Lieutenant-Colonel) Rohde of 319 Infantry Division, quickly succeeded in February by Major Zuske who was himself shortly afterwards promoted lieutenant-colonel. Hoffmann stayed on with the new management as senior staff officer and local tactical expert.

By then, the main component of the Army garrison was a truncated battalion (9, 10 and 11 Companies) of 582 Grenadier Regiment, one of the three infantry components of 319 Infantry Division. 9 Company was stationed in the central part of the Island, 10 Company in the west and 11 Company in the east including a small reserve force based in Essex Castle.

Alderney was beginning its three and a half years as a fortress command.

CHAPTER TWO

The Work Force

HOFFMANN BEGAN by building field works and siting weapon pits, strongpoints and observation posts in accordance with the general plans of his superior headquarters, to make the best use of the strength and firepower of the garrison as it increased, until such time as permanent and more elaborate concrete structures could supersede them. Many of these original sites continued in use throughout the war, and it is clear that he showed some tactical skill in their location.

The first major development towards fulfilling Hitler's Directive of October 1941 was the movement of very large stocks of cement and steel reinforcement to Alderney and the other Islands, together with a big enough work force to carry out the required construction. Those charged with the fulfilment of this task were the *Organisation Todt* (OT).

The OT was a civilian agency set up under Nazi Party (NSDAP) auspices in the 1930s to broke German and foreign labour to firms engaged on national construction projects. As the war progressed it became the administrator of a vast forced labour pool which it made available to individual contractors. It is in this capacity that we meet it in Alderney.

Although its German staff were civilians, they wore uniform (captured Czechoslovak khaki, not German military uniform), were subject to military law, and enjoyed para-military status with access to military facilities.

It is interesting to note that Dr. Fritz Todt, the founder of OT, began his engineering career in 1922 with the Munich firm Sager und Wörner and that Sager und Wörner were among the German contractors employing forced labour on the concrete works in Alderney. Also working for Sager und Wörner in the 1920s was the engineer Xaver Dorsch who left with Todt, became Director of the OT in Berlin, and lent his name to one of the pre-war inter-Island ships, the 'Staffa', which was re-named 'Xaver Dorsch' by the Germans; it was wrecked in a storm at Braye in 1943, but its remains were still visible near the west base of the jetty in Braye Harbour in 1945.

Command Structure

Control of the new defence works programme, as has already been noted, was vested in the Army, and it was exercised over the OT at two levels. The overall costs were borne by the Armed Forces Estimates. More detailed supervision of specifications on the ground was carried out by the Fortress Engineers Staff (*Festungspionierstab*), subordinated in turn to Fortress Construction Command XV in the Channel Islands, the Inspector for Western Fortifications (*Inspekteur der Westbefestigungen*) at Army Group level in Paris and, ultimately, the Ordnance Office (*Waffenamt*) in Berlin. The immediate allocation and supervision of tasks in Alderney on behalf of the Army was the responsibility of Fortress Engineers Sector Detachment (*Festungspionierabschnittsgruppe*) II/11, often referred to by the Germans simply as Fest. Pi. Stab II/11).

The OT had its own chain of command up to its Head Office (*OT-Zentrale* - OTZ) in Berlin. The Alderney Sector (*Abschnitt*), codename 'Adolf', was at first subordinated to the Chief Construction Office (*Oberbauleitung*) in St. Malo, then, from February 1943, to that in Cherbourg, both in turn being responsible to the Operations Group West (*Einsatzgruppe West*) in Paris. The switch to Cherbourg was an attempt to improve communication and sea transport.

Location

The OT set up four camps for its labour force in Alderney. Each consisted of wooden huts, erected by a volunteer force of French workmen who arrived in January 1942 and stayed until June. The first German OT staff arrived in that same month to control the camps. The OT mounted their own guard on the gates to the camps, which were surrounded by a wire fence. Each camp was called after a German North Sea island:

Helgoland Camp, also known as No 1 Camp, was built on the south side of the new concrete road laid by the Germans largely along the line of the old unmetalled road parallel to Platte Saline beach. The entrance pillars of the gateway are still standing and have been incorporated into the driveway of a post-war house built on the site. The camp housed forced labour, principally Russian, and had a maximum capacity of about 1,500.

Norderney Camp (No 2 Camp) was situated on the low ground between Saye Farm and Château à l'Étoc (known to the Germans as *Einsiedlerschloss* — Hermit's Castle), now used as a camping site, and some of the hut foundations can still be seen. It housed both Russian and European (French, Czech, Dutch, Spanish) forced labour and some German volunteers. It also had a maximum capacity of about 1,500.

Borkum Camp (No 3 Camp) was just behind Longis House, lying athwart the road leading to the Haize rubbish tip on the south cliffs. It was used throughout to house specialist craftsmen, many of them German and volunteers. Its complement fluctuated between 500 and 1,000.

Sylt Camp (No 4 Camp) was smaller, built originally by the OT to the south of the airfield, adjoining the cliff road. It was used by the OT for Russian and other forced labour from August 1942 to March 1943, when it was handed over to the SS and becomes the subject of Chapter Five. It had a capacity of 1,000, but this was not filled by the OT in the first instance.

In addition to the camps, small groups of forced labour were also billeted out on special projects, for example, the farm set up by FK 515.

Organisation

The senior OT representative resident on Alderney was the Construction Superintendent (*Bauleiter*) whose HQ (*Bauleitung*) was at Essex (now Devereux) House. His equivalent military rank would approximate to major. During the second half of 1942 and the beginning of 1943 — the period of worst conditions — the *Bauleiter* was Diploma Engineer Johann Buthmann (or Buttmann, the spelling varies); he was reported to have been court-martialled by the Germans in France later. After two brief periods between March and September 1943, the post was held by Leo Ackerman until the final withdrawal of the OT in summer 1944.

Under the *Bauleiter*'s overall authority, the camps and the labour force were administered by the *OT Frontführer*; in late 1942 and early 1943 this was Lucian Linke, followed through summer 1943 by Theo Konnertz. A Camp Commander (*Lagerführer* or *Lagerleiter*) with the rank of OT *Haupttruppführer* or *Obertruppführer*, was responsible to the *Frontführer* for each of the four (later three) camps; their equivalent military rank would approximate to warrant officer. Karl Tietz, Camp Commander of Norderney in late 1942 and early 1943, was the most notorious beater of forced labourers on the Island.

A number of further *Haupttruppführer* carried responsibility to the *Bauleiter* for the construction work carried out by each of the German firms to whom the labour was contracted by the OT. The principal firms concerned were: Deubau of Düsseldorf, based in Helgoland Camp; Fuchs of Koblenz, based in Norderney Camp; Kniffler of Saarbrücken, based in Helgoland Camp; Sager und Wörner of Munich, based in Norderney Camp; Wolfer und Goebel, based in Norderney Camp. Also conducting smaller operations in Alderney were the German firms Strabag, Westfälische Steinindustrie and Karl G. Blume, the French firm Colignon and an unidentified Dutch firm.

Various lower ranks, *OT Truppführer, OT Meister* and *OT Vorarbeiter*, corresponded roughly to descending ranks of NCO and were responsible for direct control of the work force both in and out of camp.

Numbers

The first draft of forced labourers arrived in Alderney in July 1942. It consisted of about 1,000 *'Ostarbeiter'* (Eastern European workers, i.e. Russians, Ukrainians and Poles). They were followed in August by two further drafts, each of about 900, loosely described as 'Russians', though it is to be supposed that other *'Ostarbeiter'* may have been among them. The term 'Russian' will be used in this loose way hereafter for convenience. These intakes were divided between Helgoland and Norderney Camps, with a part of the last draft going to Sylt Camp. There was also a group of between four and five hundred volunteer workers, principally Germans, housed in Borkum Camp in July.

It is difficult to give precise figures for the labour force at any one time, because there is discrepancy between different records calculated to different specifications which were often not clearly postulated. It is thus not always possible to know whether a given figure refers to OT foreign forced labour, all OT labour or all labour including (from March 1943) the concentration camp. Moreover the build-up of numbers was not a steady inflow, but fluctuated with drafts both inward and outward throughout the period. Ration strength in the official documents was not necessarily an accurate guide for, as will be seen below, the food and pay of the labour force were not honestly administered.

However, we are able to reconstruct an approximate picture of how the labour force fluctuated. Of 300 Spaniards brought to Alderney in summer 1942, almost all had been withdrawn by the end of the year. Between 700 and 800 'Russians' were shipped back to Cherbourg in January 1943. In this same month, the newly arrived OT *Haupttrupp-führer* Johann Hoffmann (no relation of Carl) gave the distribution of the forced labour force as follows:

> 'Helgoland —1,050 men of whom 150 were Germans, 900 Russians, the latter including about 220 sick marooned aboard the ship in the harbour.
>
> Norderney —900 men, a few more Germans than in Helgoland, remainder Russians with a few Frenchmen etc.
>
> Sylt —100–120 Russians
>
> There were furthermore roughly 200 Russians not in camps but dispersed on sites all over the Island. In February 1943, Helgoland received an intake of 50–60 Russians from Sylt, plus some 40–50 personnel of the firms Kniffler and Deubau from Norderney... Helgoland sent all Sager und Wörner personnel to Norderney in February–March 1943...
>
> When the OT Camp Sylt was dissolved (March 1943), about half the 100-120 men in that camp were transferred to Helgoland and half to Norderney.'

In May 1943, the German records for the Channel Islands as a whole listed a grand total of 4,000 workers in Alderney; this would presumably include the recently arrived concentration camp.

In September, the breakdown of OT workers only was given (approximate figures) as:

> 700 Russians in Helgoland Camp
> 400 volunteer workers of various European nationalities
> 100 women, mostly French
> 300 French Jews in Norderney Camp
> 700 German OT workers located as follows:
>> 400 in Borkum Camp
>> 150 in Helgoland Camp
>> 150 in Norderney Camp

This tallies well with *Bauleiter* Ackermann's statement to the author in 1945:

> 'By order of the Commander of the OT *Oberbauleitung* Cherbourg, I went to Alderney on 20 August 1943 and took over the *Bauleitung* in Alderney from 1 September. At this time I found the following disposition of personnel on Alderney:
> 1. Almost 700 German OT workers
> 2. Almost 1,500 foreign OT workers
> 3. About 700 concentration camp prisoners of the SS *Baubrigade*
> Only the German and foreign workers indicated by 1 and 2 above were under my command.'

There were 27 different nationalities represented in the labour force on Alderney in the course of the period.

In autumn 1943, the evacuation of the remaining Russians to Cherbourg began. According to Johann Hoffmann:

> 'Between September/October 1943 and January 1944, all the Russians except about 20 were evacuated from Helgoland Camp. Even before that date, most of the German personnel had left and the remainder was reduced to about 40. In March 1944, Helgoland Camp was disbanded and transferred to Norderney.'

Helgoland Camp was then destroyed.

As a partial replacement for the loss of Russian labour, there arrived on the Island in October 1943 an intake of 250 French Jews and 150 civilian prisoners, all of whom were accommodated in Norderney. Johann Hoffmann continues:

> 'In Norderney Camp almost all the Russians were withdrawn between September/October 1943 and January 1944. In June

1944, after the invasion, all the Jews, Frenchmen and Moroccans were evacuated.'

Apart from a few individuals, all non-German OT workers had been evacuated from Alderney by July 1944 and Norderney Camp was destroyed.

Sylt Camp after March 1943 is discussed in Chapter Five below.

CHAPTER THREE

Conditions of Work

FOREIGN WORKERS in the forced labour contingents, with certain exceptions like the Jews and civilian prisoners who arrived in October 1943, were in theory volunteers. Some of the Russians, for example, had been invited to volunteer for agricultural work in France. The Spaniards had been given the option of work on military construction sites or being returned to Franco's Spain, from which they were Republican refugees in France. The degree of compulsion in recruitment varied, but the conditions under which they were held and employed may justify their own description of themselves as forced labour.

Apart from that small minority fortunate enough to be assigned to special projects where conditions were easier, the norm was 12 hours heavy manual work a day, sometimes longer, for seven days a week. The exceptions to this timetable were a daily lunch break, varying between ten and forty minutes, and a half day's holiday on one Sunday in the month. When night shifts were worked, the day was free and the on-site 'lunch-meal' was served during the night.

Forced labourers had no right to complain about their hours or conditions of work.

In theory forced labourers were entitled to pay at the rate of 55 *Reichspfennig* per hour. But, as *Frontführer* Johann Hoffmann (he was promoted to succeed Konnertz) explained:

> '55 per cent of this was deducted at source as the so-called Eastern Levy (*Ostabgabe*), a compulsory contribution for the reconstruction of destroyed areas in Eastern Europe. Of the rest, 55 Pfennig per day was supposed to be paid out in cash, however I found that this was never done.'

He went on to say how he eventually managed to get these outstanding sums credited on paper to those forced labourers to whom they were due, but added wryly: 'I am sure that in many cases these credits have never been paid out'.

The forced labourers were in general not issued with clothing. Wooden sabots were sometimes exchanged for shoes when the latter wore out, failing which the feet were wrapped in rags; in 1943, some worn and torn clothing was made available in certain cases as a replacement. For the rest, they wore what they had been wearing at the moment of their conscription or engagement, which for many was the summer of 1941 in Eastern Europe. They thus went through the winter of 1942–43 in Alderney in thin cotton clothing which had been constantly in use for over a year and was often in tatters. The tatterdemalion appearance of these unfortunates was the subject of some comment among the troops of the garrison, sometimes in ribald jest and sometimes with compassion. The true measure of the reality of their plight is perhaps conveyed by two facts on the record. Many of the Germans mentioned how the first thing that happened when a dead forced labourer was found was that he was stripped naked by his nearest mates. eager to augment their own scant wardrobe. And the records of a careful, book-keeping administration noted time and again that a forced labourer had died 'possessed of no effects whatever'.

There was no proper medical treatment available to the forced labourers. The two successive OT doctors, who were responsible from the opening of the camps in 1942 until July 1943, made no proper medical inspection either of the camps or of their occupants. After mid-1943, OT medical interests were represented, nominally as far as the forced labourers were concerned, by the naval medical officer on the Island.

The decision whether or not a camp inmate should be allowed to report sick rested with the OT Camp Commanders, who on occasion beat up the sick parade if they thought it was too large. If a man were suffering from physical accident, say a broken arm, he stood a better chance of acceptance on the sick list than if he were constitutionally ill, unless he was actually incapable of work.

During the winter of 1942–43, when the casualty rate was highest, the OT doctors showed little or no interest in the forced labourers. Simple cases in Helgoland Camp were 'treated' by a German medical orderly; for transfer to the sick-bay in Norderney Camp he would only accept stretcher cases. The sick-bay at Norderney was run by a Russian émigré doctor from France, assisted by a French nurse and two Russian orderlies but without proper medical facilities; more sinister still, admission was only by leave of a German OT NCO (non-medical).

There is no evidence that any constitutionally sick foreign forced labourer working for the OT ever received proper medical attention on Alderney or was sent from Alderney to receive it elsewhere.

Brutality

Arbitrary beatings by OT staff were a daily occurrence in Helgoland and Norderney Camps. They were carried out with fist, foot, stick, piece of hosepipe or other weapon. The reasons given were for trivial breaches of the harsh regulations, and often there was no palpable reason at all. Let some of the victims who survived speak for themselves:

> 'Every day the Camp Commander made a habit of beating any man he found not standing properly to attention or who had not made his bed properly or did not execute a drill movement properly. The beatings were carried out on the head, face or body with a stick about 2½ centimetres in diameter. The Camp Commander's assistant also beat workers daily with a stick of the same thickness on all parts of the body until their faces were covered with blood and they could not rise from the ground, when he would call on the prisoner's mates to carry the prostrate body away.'

And again:

> 'In October 1942, there was an occasion when a carrot was thrown from a window by one of the cooks and was picked up outside by a Russian who was beaten mercilessly with a stick and then kicked while lying on the ground.'

Thus a Pole and a Russian, two of many, describing their daily life in Norderney Camp. It was no better at Helgoland:

> 'If ever a man was reported to the Camp Commander for taking food from the garbage pails, he would summon the offender to his office, beat him with a stick or length of rubber hose filled with sand until he fell to the ground, kick him and order him to leave the office.'

Lagerleiter Ludwig Becker of Helgoland was not all that much of an improvement on Karl Tietz of Norderney.

Sylt offered the same experience. One Pole (a forced labourer, not a political prisoner) recorded:

> '[The *Truppführer*] gave an order to cut ten sticks on which they then fitted rubber tubes. Then we were beaten with them. Very often we were beaten without reason; sometimes we were accused of laziness; but mostly we were beaten out of hatred. They called us 'Communist swine' * and 'bloody Poles' etc. Often the men were beaten so long that they fell down from sheer weakness . . . We were beaten every day.
>
> 'My friend Antoni Onuchowski died that way. He was from my native village and of course I knew him very well. Onuchowski

*This is evidence of the same attitude of mind that entered on some of the OT Forms: 'Nationality: Bolshevik'.

had stayed behind in Sylt Camp for a few days because of illness. He had swollen feet. Afterwards he got a bit better, but he was still very weak and could not walk properly. One day, after work, when our squad was marching back to camp, he could not keep up and fell behind. I saw the *Truppführer* remain with him and get to work with his truncheon. Later we lost sight of him. All the evening we kept waiting in the camp for him, but he never returned. The next morning after reveille, when I went to the latrine, Onuchowski lay there on the other side of the barbed wire at the side of the camp. His face was covered with red weals and when we later brought his body into the camp and undressed it, we could distinctly see the weals and blotches on his body.'

Onuchowski's death was listed as taking place on 28 September 1942.

Part of the perspective in which all this brutality should be viewed may be seen in the case of Karl Tietz. Tietz was the Camp Commander first of Sylt and then, late on 1942, of Norderney. He had the reputation among his charges of being the most brutal of all their OT overseers. He picked a sturdy French negro and trained him to do camp floggings for him. Tietz was court-martialed by the Germans in April 1943 and sentenced to one year and six months penal servitude — not for his treatment of the inmates of his camps, but for black marketeering in cigarettes and illegal 'purchase' of watches and other valuables from some of the Dutch inmates.

Diet

Normal meals during the autumn and winter of 1942 — that is, before there was any question of short supply caused by Allied blockade of the Channel Islands — consisted of:

Breakfast —½ litre of coffee substitute, without milk or sugar. This was consumed in camp before going out to work.

Lunch   —½ litre of thin cabbage or other vegetable soup. This was served at the working site and known as 'Bunker-suppe' (Bunker soup).

Supper   —½ litre of similar soup and a 1 kilo loaf of bread to be shared among 5–6 men. This was eaten in camp. In theory the bread was for use at breakfast next day also.

In addition, 25 grammes of butter per head were issued twice (sometimes three times) a week, and on isolated occasions a portion of sausage, jam, cheese or fresh vegetable. There was never any meat or sugar until 1944, when most of the OT workers had left Alderney.

Inevitably this malnutrition led to attempts by individual forced labourers to acquire additional food, and the majority of cases where they were shot by sentries were on this account. It also accounted for some deaths by poisoning from eating deadly nightshade berries and smoking dried bracken.

The failure to feed the work force at subsistence level was what happened in practice on the ground in 1942 and most of 1943. It is, of course, not reflected in the theory or the book-keeping, and it may be necessary to look at this in more detail to see where the responsibility lay.

The ration scales for the Armed Forces and forced labourers in the Channel Islands were laid down by the Quartermaster's Branch (IV A) of the staff of HQ 319 Infantry Division. Until the end of 1942, the troops were on Scale III and the forced labourers on Scale IV; the principal difference between these two scales was that Scale III gave 800 grammes of meat a week and 700 grammes of bread daily, while Scale IV gave 100 grammes less in each case. From some time in 1943 on, the troops' ration went up to Scale II and the forced labourers went on to a scale between III and IV — basically Scale III without certain items described as luxuries like pulses and farinaceous foods. It was specified that officers and men were to receive the same ration in the Armed Forces but that the German OT personnel were to receive the military scale and their work force the lower scale.

Alderney was supplied as a whole from 319 Divisional Supply Sub-depots at Granville and Cherbourg. The Army broke bulk on the Island and handed the OT its entitlement according to the prescribed scale at the time and its ration strength. There was a local Army Supply Dump on Alderney in which an attempt was made to keep a standing reserve of up to 3 months' basic requirements.

There was no complaint by the OT to the Army that rations were delivered short or late, and indeed it was standard Army practice to allow a generous percentage for wastage of perishables and to offset any momentary shortage of one commodity by an equivalent increase in another: for example, the standard ration under Scale II, III and IV was 1400 grammes of potato and 1200 grammes of vegetable daily per man; if potatoes were deficient, the shortfall was made up by vegetables of a calculated equal calorific value.

The forced labourers' rations appear to have been gravely mis-appropriated at two separate levels. On the Army side, two quarter-master officers, *Oberzahlmeister* (Lieutenant) Frank and *Oberzahlmeister* Krüger were on several occasions accused of diverting supplies for their own ends. No case was, however, brought against them until June 1944. Krüger was degraded to the rank of private soldier in April 1945 and Frank committed suicide.

On the OT side, those responsible for receiving bulk ration issues from the Army in Alderney in 1942 and the first half of 1943 were OT *Haupttruppführer* Helling and OT *Haupttruppführer* Standop. They were in charge of the OT Central Supply Depot (*Zentralverpflegungslager* — ZVL) on the Island. They were accused in 1943 of misappropriating rations: not, as one might perhaps have supposed, for failing to issue the rations to which the work force was entitled, but for overindenting by 600 heads over actual ration strength and selling the surplus for personal profit. Both were posted from the Island in summer 1943, Standop to stand trial in Berlin and Helling to 2 years' penal servitude on conviction by a 319 Infantry Division court-martial; he died in August 1943 in Aschendorfer Moor Penal Camp in the Emsland, where he was reported to have committed suicide.

The significant feature of life in practice in the undernourished labour force was, as one inmate put it:

> 'Within a month and a half of my arrival at Norderney Camp the average death rate was 2–3 per day. At the time of our arrival we had all been in normal health, but constant beatings and starvation diet had reduced us to an extremely feeble condition.'

In the words of one compassionate Austrian NCO in the 3rd Company of Engineer Construction Battalion (*Baupionierbataillon*) 158 billeted opposite the slaughterhouse:

> 'If those men wanted to rest owing to fatigue, they were beaten by OT NCOs in charge of the working parties with sticks and spade handles. If a man could even then not carry on, he was threatened with stoppage of food . . . . They were thus forced to obtain their means of subsistence some other way. I have seen undernourished Russian workers forced by hunger digging up with their bare hands the buried intestines of slaughtered animals behind the slaughterhouse in order to satisfy their hunger.'

(The remains of the monogram of this NCO's unit can still be seen in the concrete at the Fort end of the Clonque causeway, against the date 'I.XII.42'.)

The extremity to which forced labourers were reduced by hunger is further illustrated by the case of two Russians shot by a sentry below a minefield on the south cliffs. In the words of the military police warrant officer who investigated the incident:

> 'Both bodies showed signs of the chest and stomach wounds causing death . . . . I could only establish that the two Russians had been living in a cave nearby, as I found there straw beds and a supply of mussels which the Russians had collected for themselves. I supposed they had been caught while looking for mussels.'

They would, of course, have had to eat the mussels raw.

If dishonest misappropriation was one contributory cause of their plight, deliberate inhumanity was another.

From the beginning the garrison was forbidden to give any food to the forced labourers. The standing order of Lieutenant-Colonel Zuske, the Island Commandant, was read out regularly on parade to all units:

> 'I hereby forbid the employment of any Russians except those especially designated, and further forbid the giving of bread or any other foodstuffs to them. Unit commanders are responsible to me for compliance with this order.'

The extant copy of this order was dated 9 October 1942, but there is reference to another version as early as 19 August 1942.

And those who did not comply were indeed punished. But there remained nevertheless some officers and men who did not comply, and at least one commanding officer who punished the offence with only a token sentence: three days' restrictive arrest for giving a starving Russian a 1½ kilo loaf of bread.

When eventually an inspection of Helgoland and Norderney was ordered by an uneasy higher authority, the Island Commandant, Zuske, made do with a superficial affair. No questions were asked and the report was anodyne and not even in writing.

The rations issued to forced labourers appear to have improved slightly after summer 1943. Just how difficult it was to effect any improvement at all in the climate obtaining is perhaps illustrated by Johann Hoffmann who took over as Commander of Helgoland Camp in January 1943 and replaced Konnertz as OT *Frontführer* in November of that year:

> 'As early as the first 8 days after my arrival I made verbal complaints to *Frontführer* Lucian Linke and *Bauleiter* Buttmann. Complaints in writing were contained in my monthly report for February. My complaints concerned insufficient food and bad accommodation.
> 'Linke maintained that in general it was my business as Camp Commander to make ends meet with existing stocks and deliveries. Regarding the question of billets, Buttmann declared that concreting had priority over all other works on the Island and regarding the question of food, "he would see". A little later, when visiting Helgoland, Linke complained *to me* that the numbers of sick had increased at Helgoland since my arrival. I replied that more people were reported sick because it was not my habit to send people out to work by beating them without regard to their state of health. Again I complained to Linke because of the insufficient food and again he replied that I did

not know how to make do with the quantity available . . .

'Possibly not so many of them would have died if they had been accommodated better. In the first place the huts were set too low in the ground and there were walls of earth almost up to the roof, thrown up during the excavation. So they were dark and not properly ventilated . . . . The huts had no concrete foundations, they rested only on short props. Consequently during the winter months damp would penetrate through the floor boards which could not be counteracted by the two stoves in the hut nor had the men a chance to dry their wet clothes properly . . .

'The huts were on average 20–30 metres long, 7 metres wide and about 3 metres high. They were French Army huts. When I arrived, they housed between 90 and 100 men each. I reduced this to 80 and in the summer 1943 to 70 men per hut. There were only bunks in double tiers with rather thinly filled palliasses and, in most cases, one blanket per man. They were entitled to three blankets and at least I managed to procure them a second blanket each.'

In spite of Hoffmann's statement, some of the huts nevertheless only had one stove (for 100 men). It was not permitted to light the stoves until the outside work gangs had returned to camp in the evening, usually between 7 and 8 pm, and fires had to be put out either at 11 pm or midnight, it varied.

It is important to see the philosophy of a totalitarian regime like the Third Reich (there are, of course, others to whom it also applies) at work in the selection and treatment of forced labour. It may otherwise be hard for us to understand the apparent illogic of starving and working to death one's construction labour force. A German NCO on Alderney echoed this bewilderment over what he saw:

'I could never understand why the Russians were fed as they were, because at that time we had as much as we wanted to eat. I used to give them bread myself because I felt sorry for them. I have a large family and I know what hunger means.'

But once people are labelled sub-human, are written off as of no value and no longer really count, then the illogic begins to disappear. They could, after all, be replaced.

Evacuation

Any improvement in conditions was only relative, it would seem. 180 sick Russians were transported to Cherbourg on the 'Franka' in January 1943. A further 300 Russians were due to be evacuated to Cherbourg later in the same month on the 'Xaver Dorsch', and an Able Seaman working in the Harbour Commandant's office described what he saw as follows:

'The ship stayed in the harbour of Alderney for three days after the Russians had been loaded. The men were crowded together in its holds like herrings, without straw, beds, blankets or benches. They were terribly emaciated. We had to carry their food from the harbour to the ship once daily during those three days. I myself took part in each of those three trips on boat FF 08 of the Harbour Guard Unit. The food was in buckets containing a watery soup with some vegetables in it. They received no bread. When opening the hatches to the holds, a terrible stench would meet us. On the return journey on each occasion we had to take with us frightfully emaciated corpses of the Russians — over the 3 days 8 to 10 bodies all told.'

It was at this time that the 'Xaver Dorsch' was wrecked at Braye with some further loss of life. The remaining cargo of forced labourers was transferred to the 'Franka' and evacuated to Cherbourg.

A similar draft of forced labourers was freighted out in October 1943 on board the 'Dorothea Weber', in equally poor conditions. There was, it is true, no shipwreck, but the men were kept under battened hatches for 36 hours without food before sailing from Braye Harbour.

The final withdrawal of the residue of the OT labour force took place after the Allied invasion of Normandy. It was effected in July 1944, to St. Malo.

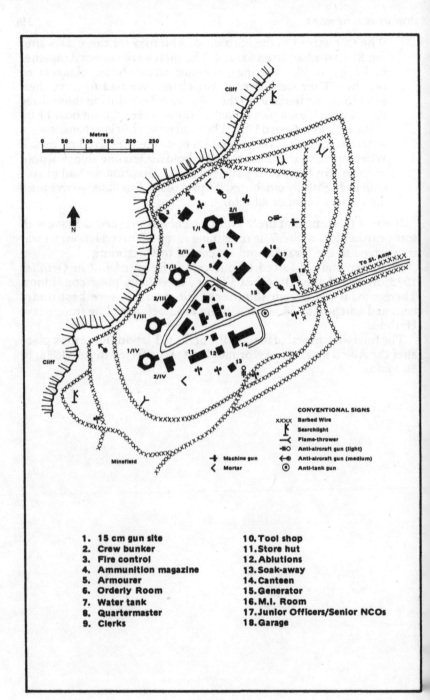

CONVENTIONAL SIGNS

xxxx	Barbed Wire
	Searchlight
	Flame-thrower
	Anti-aircraft gun (light)
	Anti-aircraft gun (medium)
	Anti-tank gun
+ Machine gun	
Mortar	

1. 15 cm gun site
2. Crew bunker
3. Fire control
4. Ammunition magazine
5. Armourer
6. Orderly Room
7. Water tank
8. Quartermaster
9. Clerks
10. Tool shop
11. Store hut
12. Ablutions
13. Soak-away
14. Canteen
15. Generator
16. M.I. Room
17. Junior Officers/Senior NCOs
18. Garage

Westbatterie

CHAPTER FOUR

The Hardware

WHAT WAS the vast work force building emplacements for?

Coastal Defence

The new military role in which Alderney was cast from 1941 was planned to give a modest offensive strike capacity as well as high defensive potential. Hitler's long term plans for the Channel Islands and the immediate tactical requirements of the war he had not yet won both needed the ability to control the sea approaches to Alderney and the passage between Alderney and France by means of strong coastal artillery based on the island.

Three batteries of medium coastal artillery were constructed, two of which were manned by the Navy and one by the Army. Fire control was eventually in a new, tall concrete tower on Mannez Hill, overlooking the northern and eastern shores of the Island and equipped with radar; it is still a prominent feature of the skyline.

On the Giffoine, at the north-west corner of the Island, was a battery of 4 x 15 cm SK C/28 guns manned by a naval artillery unit, *Marineartillerieabteilung* (MAA) 605. The open gun pits in concrete can still be seen, together with the magazines and quarters for the crews on duty beneath them and the ammunition hoists. Adjacent are the underground concrete bunkers for the gun crews not on duty, the site for the rangefinder and neighbouring searchlight and local defence positions. In keeping with other major sites on Alderney still to be mentioned, this battery had its own capacity to generate electricity, its own water supply, workshop, armoury, essential storage and recreation hut. The official name of this position was the *Batterie St Annes* or *Westbatterie*, but it was universally known to the troops as *'Batterie Annes'* (two syllables).

Fort Albert, known by the Germans as *Albertsburg* or *Burg Albert*, and later as *Dollmannfeste* (Dollmann Fortress) after Colonel-General Friedrich Dollmann, commanding general of the 7th Army in France, was the headquarters of MAA 605. It was one of a dozen-odd Victorian forts adapted by the Germans to their more immediate purposes. Also in Fort Albert was a battery of 3 x 17.26 cm SK L/40 guns, the heaviest coastal artillery on Alderney. They were so sited as to give an all round coverage of fire. The code name for this position was *Batterie Elsass* (Alsace).

The third medium battery was situated on the high ground south of the Longis Road and east of the track leading southward from the Hèche to Cachalière. It consisted of 4 x 15 cm K18 guns in open gun pits and was manned by an Army coastal artillery unit *Heeresküstenbatterie* 461. There was 'Freya' type radar on this site. The battery was commanded from Balmoral House in the Longis Road, in the garden of which was mounted a rangefinder on a wooden tower. The code name for this whole position was *Batterie Blücher*.

There were two other coastal artillery batteries on Alderney, both mounting light calibre guns.

On the site of the old Roselle Battery, west of Fort Albert at the eastern lip of the harbour mouth, were 4 x 10.5 cm former French K331(f) guns in casemates, also manned by MAA 605. This battery was known to the Germans as the *Rosenbatterie* (Rose Battery) — no doubt a not very imaginative adaptation of Roselle. In connection with this position, a number of small and medium calibre weapons and a searchlight were sited on Bibette Head, at the entrance to the harbour. The *Rosenbatterie* appears to have led a chequered life and to have been manned by a variety of crews in the latter stages of the war, taken from other units and trained on the job. From July 1944, this position was known as the *Batterie General Marcks*, after General Erich Marcks, commander of LXXXIV Corps, who was killed in action near St Lô shortly after the Allied invasion of Normandy.

A second light battery was situated on the high ground east of *Batterie Blücher*. It consisted of a troop (11/319 A.R.) of 10 cm light howitzers of Czech origin (le FH14/19(t)) from 319 divisional artillery regiment, in open emplacements in a coastal defence role. The codename for this position was *Batterie Falke* (Falcon).

In addition to these batteries, individual guns were sited at tactically significant points to contribute to coastal defence. Many of them were captured French 10.5 cm guns, K.331(f) said to have been brought to the Island in June 1942. They were located as follows, mainly in concrete bunkers:

10.5 cm Coast Defence Guns (casemated) K.331(f)

Fort Clonque	south-west	1 gun
(known to the Germans as *Steinfeste:* Stone Fort)		
Fort Tourgis	south-west	1 gun
	north-east	1 gun
Fort Grosnez	south-west	1 gun
	north-east	1 gun
Roselle	north-west	4 guns
Bibette	south-west	1 gun
Quesnard*	north-west	1 gun
Raz Island	north-east	1 gun
(known to the Germans as	south-west	1 gun
Eilandfeste: Island Fort)		

Cachalière	south-west	1 gun

*Ground slab only completed

   10.5 cm Coast Defence Guns (field positions)   2 guns

Anti-landing defences also included two 5 cm M.19 automatic mortars mounted in bunkers situated in the Bonne Terre east of Fort Tourgis, and to the east of Mannez Hill. These are the only two such sites to survive intact in the Channel Islands.

Anti-aircraft defence

In a defensive role, the anti-aircraft and anti-tank artillery were deployed on an equally lavish scale. It should be remembered in this context that the standard German heavy AA gun, 8.8 cm, was designed as a dual-purpose weapon which could also be employed against ground targets. Except for a small number of Army and Navy units, the AA artillery of the German Armed Forces were normally manned by the Air Force.

The AA contingent on Alderney was a mixed force consisting of four troops (*Batterien*, in German terminology) each of 4 x 8.8 cm heavy AA guns (*Fliegerabwehrkanonen*, FLAK) supported by a variable number of light 2 cm AA guns mounted singly, in pairs (*Zwillinge*, twins) or in fours (*Vierlinge*, quadruplets).

One troop was situated on the Giffoine just north-east of the *Westbatterie*, on the cliffs above Fort Clonque. Another was at Les Auteuils on the edge of the airfield, south-west of the Marette. A third was sited just south of the fire control tower on Mannez Hill, in concrete gun pits which are still very much in evidence and readily accessible today; this troop shot down a Flying Fortress in March 1943. Finally, there was a fourth troop on the cliff top just south-west of Essex Castle. As with the coastal artillery, each of these major AA sites had administrative and storage facilities on site, albeit on a smaller scale, and was protected by its own local defence positions.

There were also a number of 2 cm or 3.7 cm light AA troops sited separately — on the Tête de Judemarre, above Telegraph Bay, on the Little Blaye, on the edge of the Butes, on York Hill, at Château à l'Étoc and beside Simon's Place. In addition some 2 cm light AA guns were individually sited at small vulnerable points, for example, at the base and tip of the breakwater and at the base of the stone jetty in the harbour.

A number of the AA troop positions included searchlights. There were also radars on the Giffoine, at the bungalow above Fort Tourgis, and above the Vau Renier; the crew for the latter was for a time quartered at 'Quatre Vents', known to the troops as 'The Millionaire's House' (*Das Millionärhaus*).

Anti-tank defences

Apart from the 8.8 cm AA guns already mentioned in a dual role, the anti-tank defences of Alderney really fell into two categories: the defended obstacles on the exposed beaches; and isolated weapons sited to hinder the passage of any armoured vehicles that might penetrate beyond, towards the interior of the Island.

The two beaches judged by the Germans to be most vulnerable to a seaborne landing by armoured vehicles were Platte Saline and Longis Bay — known to the Germans as *Lange Bucht* (Long Bay). They built a not wholly successful stretch of experimental wall on the former, but the latter was protected by a formidable ferro-concrete obstacle calculated to deny any landed vehicle exit from the beach.

Other, less vulnerable, beaches were mined and wired, and on some tetroid metal obstacles were erected, known in German military parlance as *'Igel'* (Hedgehogs), for example, at the gap in the Longis Wall and on both sides of the Raz Island causeway, beside the Douglas Quay at Braye, at Saye and Arch Bays, and on Platte Saline (where a few can still be seen). Steel rails were used between concrete posts to bar narrow gaps where the causeway cuts the Longis Wall and where the Clonque Road rounds the base of Fort Tourgis.

The beach obstacles were covered by anti-tank guns in casemates built on the edges of the bays or into the sea walls:

7.5 cm Anti-Tank Guns (casemated) Pak 40		
Clonque Bay	west	1 gun
Longis Bay	south	1 gun
4.7 cm Anti-Tank Guns (casemated) Pak (t)		
Fort Doyle	south-west	1 gun
Fort Grosnez	north-east	1 gun
Nunnery	east	1 gun
4.7 Anti-Tank Guns (field positions)		6 guns
5 cm Anti-Tank Guns (casemated) Pak 38		
Braye	east	1 gun
5 cm Anti-Tank Guns (field positions)		5 guns

These were sometimes supported by fire from those further away, eg two on the higher ground above Braye and Crabby Bays respectively and one on the north-western edge of the Butes.

Isolated individual guns covered key roadways, eg a formidable turret at ground level, entered only from below, at the bend in the Braye Road covered both upper and lower reaches of the main access road to the harbour.

Armoured Vehicles

The Germans had a mobile reserve of between twelve and fifteen armoured vehicles on Alderney. The majority were obsolete Renault light tanks, captured from the French. One or two may have been captured Czech vehicles.

The tanks were distributed in three separate parks, obviously chosen to facilitate the easy deployment of the vehicles in emergency. One park was just off the Rose Farm Road. The second was in St Martins. The third was in hutments adjoining Longis House.

Mines

In principle, the Germans laid a ring of land mines and barbed wire round the perimeter of the Island. It ran along the cliff-top—and sometimes down the cliff—along the whole south side of the Island from Essex Castle to a point above Fort Clonque, and then on the landward side of the beaches and rocks around the other, northern side. Narrow exits were left open for necessary passage through the barrier, eg on Corblets and Braye Bays, for bathing parties. In more vulnerable areas such as the low ground between Fort Albert and Longis Bay, minefields were laid inland, as also they were to give all round defence to sites of particular tactical importance like the *Westbatterie*.

There are discrepant figures for the total of mines laid. The German engineer officer responsible for clearing them under British auspices in 1945 quoted 37,000 to the author, but this is more than the documentary evidence suggests. A German mine chart, prepared by the First Company of Engineer Battalion (*Pionierbataillon*) 319 in the second half of 1944, lists the individual sites which add up to a total of just under 27,000 laid from 1941 to that date.

The Royal Engineers' map of May 1945 again lists the individual sites, adding up to a total of just under 30,000 — or just over 30,000 if air-landing obstacles are included. This latter figure seems the best evidence, though the exact figure may to some extent depend on what is defined as a mine.

The two main categories of mine were anti-tank mines and anti-personnel mines. The former, chiefly *Teller* (plate) mines, so called because of their shape, were laid on road verges, in defiles and as part of the defence of anti-tank obstacles; they formed perhaps one sixth of the total. The latter, perhaps something over half the total, were widely sown on the landward side of beaches, along the cliff-tops and sides, in defence of vulnerable fortified positions and in parts of the open ground between Fort Albert and Berry's Quarry. Some were activated by direct pressure and some by tension fuses released by tripwire. Some were improvised, some were captured stocks, but the standard German anti-personnel mine was the 'S' (for *Schützen*, infantryman) mine. Its engaging peculiarity was to jump about one metre into the air on release of a depressed spring and explode a few feet away from the target that had set it off, scattering shrapnel at about navel level.

All these minefields were recorded on sketch maps in scrupulous detail — as indeed were dummy minefields, but in a different colour —, were enclosed by barbed wire fences and were clearly marked by signboards carrying a skull (with or without crossbones) and the legend: '*Achtung! Minen*'.

It may be interesting at this point to give verbatim the description given by an eyewitness in April 1943 of the wire and minefield on the landward side of Braye Beach:

'Minefield enclosed by barbed wire front and back. The wire is fixed on angle-iron posts with a square flat base welded to the posts. This is buried about two feet down, leaving four feet projecting. The posts are 10-12 feet apart. Each post has a couple of barbed stanchions. The wire between posts is barbed and the strands are nine inches apart. At intervals there are warning boards with black letters on white fields. There is evidence of tripwires in the mined area. The angle-iron posts of the barbed wire get knocked down occasionally by the sea. The beach in front of this mine belt is not mined and it is possible to walk all round Braye Beach. There is a gap in the minefield for bathers to get to the beach. They have to walk in single file through the gap which is clearly marked by wire on both sides.'

The same was not always true of those mines, whether of standard design or improvised, which were laid in the sand of the beaches and therefore liable to movement by the sea. It is these that have re-appeared from time to time in the immediate post-war years.

Improvised mines were usually explosive charges formed by lashing a number of captured (for example, French) shells together with a detonator. This might be directly triggered by pressure or tension fuse, or might be activated by remote control from a neighbouring manned position. Some of these devices were incorporated in the defences of the land approaches to the harbour area. Others were buried in beaches where, because of their heavy weight, they had to be installed by rolling them down rails, the last section of which was often buried with them, so that the protruding end of a rail might be the first sign of a *fougasse* of this type. Some were also used as extra mines in the cliff-top area adjoining the airfield.

Air-landing defences

From the very beginning, the Germans viewed Alderney's airfield not as a potential facility to be used by their own aircraft, but rather as a hazard that might invite unwelcome visitors. They guarded it defens-ively, and in time erected poles to discourage landing. Some parts of the airfield not used for Sylt Camp or other works were mined.

The area where the Germans were most frightened of airborne landing as the war wore on was Longis Common. Here they not only erected poles but wired them to explosive charges so that a given pressure on the overhead wires between the poles would detonate surrounding charges in the ground.

All in all, quite a load of hardware for a little island.

CHAPTER FIVE

The Concentration Camp

IN MARCH 1943, the OT administration handed over Sylt Camp to SS Construction Brigade I (SS *Baubrigade* I).

The SS (*Schutzstaffel*) was a para-military organ of the National Socialist Party (NSDAP), subordinated to its own commander, *Reichsführer* Heinrich Himmler. Himmler carried responsibility for it at both ministerial and party level. It was thus in no way under the jurisdiction of OKW. There was in the war years an SS field army contingent of combat troops, the *Waffen-SS*, who fought alongside the Army in their own formations, that is in separate SS divisions, but it is not these *Waffen-SS* who concern us here. The SS who manned the concentration camp on Alderney and ran *Baubrigade* I were all from the Death's Head formation (*Totenkopfverband* — TK) of the SS proper, responsible for all concentration camps both in Germany or in occupied territory — in Buchenwald, in Auschwitz or in Alderney. (This *Totenkopfverband* is not to be confused with the *Totenkopf* Division of the *Waffen-SS*, which latter had a purely military role and no connection with Alderney.)

In September 1942, the SS had decided to form a mobile construction unit from concentration camp labour. Its initial purpose was to assist on dangerous assignments in Germany, bomb disposal, rescue work and clearance after air raids. Accordingly about 1,000 inmates of the concentration camp at Sachsenhausen, near Berlin, became SS *Baubrigade* I. About 500 were Russian prisoners of war or partisans; 200 Germans classed as work-shy (*arbeitsscheu*) including conscientious objectors, habitual criminals or political prisoners, a number of whom were former members of the International Brigade in Spain; and the balance a mixed bag of political prisoners from Czechoslovakia, France, Holland and Poland.

The SS staff to guard and administer them were taken from the SS *Totenkopf* unit at the concentration camp at Neuengamme, near Hamburg, which remained the parent unit. The Brigade was stationed half in Duisburg and half in Düsseldorf from September 1942 to March 1943, when both halves were transferred to Alderney. Thereafter the whole was known as the SS Construction Brigade West, or for Abroad (SS *Baubrigade West* or SS *Baubrigade für das Ausland*).

The prisoners were transported from St Malo to Alderney on board the 'Robert Müller 8', 532 men on 3 March and 495 on 5 March.

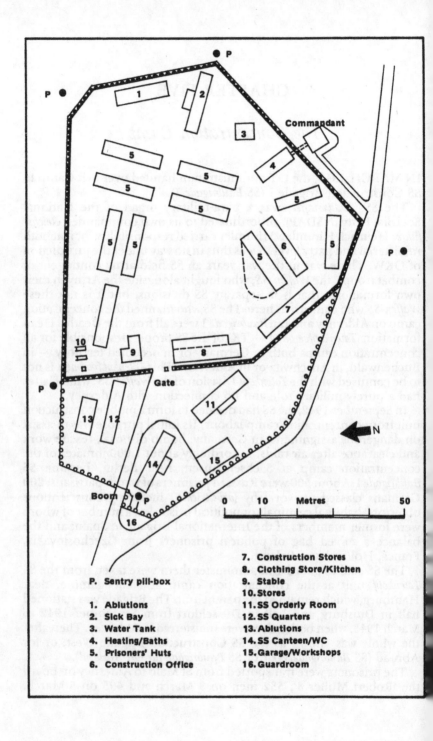

P

● **P.** Sentry pill-box

1. **Ablutions**
2. **Sick Bay**
3. **Water Tank**
4. **Heating/Baths**
5. **Prisoners' Huts**
6. **Construction Office**

7. **Construction Stores**
8. **Clothing Store/Kitchen**
9. **Stable**
10. **Stores**
11. **SS Orderly Room**
12. **SS Quarters**
13. **Ablutions**
14. **SS Canteen/WC**
15. **Garage/Workshops**
16. **Guardroom**

Commandant

Gate

N

Boom

0   10   **Metres**   50

Despite protests by the Master, Captain Hinrichsen, he was compelled to carry them in closed holds with an air space of only 2½ cubic metres per man and without water or sanitation.

Last to disembark in Alderney were the six bloodhounds — their guard dogs.

Organisation

As one might expect, the security of Sylt Camp had to be raised to a higher specification to satisfy the new masters. The camp was split into a heavily wired inner compound, which housed the prisoners, and an outer compound for the administrative staff and guards behind a token fence. A number of concrete sentry posts were erected round the perimeter, which are still visible, as is the concrete guardroom built below ground level.

The Commandant, SS *Hauptsturmführer* (Captain) Maximilian List, was an experienced hand from Neuengamme. Born on 9 February 1910, he was by civilian profession an architect. He was decorated for services performed in the Occupied Eastern Territories after the invasion of Russia in 1941. He left Neuengamme to run the Duisburg half of the *Baubrigade* and then, on transfer to Alderney, took overall command. List had a châlet built for his own quarters, just outside the perimeter wire, and an underground passage communicating with the ablutions hut in the camp, so that he could come and go without fuss. The outer end of this passage and the foundations of the châlet are still visible in the undergrowth above the spring at the top of the Val de l'Emauve.

Lists's two chief henchmen were SS *Obersturmführer* (Lieutenants) Klebeck and Braun, officers of the same stamp as their Commandant. Klebeck was List's deputy until he was posted back to Neuengamme later in 1943. Braun succeeded List as Commandant of the Alderney camp when List was posted to Oslo in Spring 1944. Braun was certified an uncured syphilitic by the senior German medical officer on Alderney.

Under the overall supervision of Klebeck as executive officer, SS *Hauptscharführer* (Warrant Officer) Otto Högelow commanded the camp staff. He came from Poland and had the advantage of speaking fluent Polish. His guard detachment, commanded by *Unterscharführer* (Corporal) Hartwig, were about half '*Reichsdeutsche*', that is, from within the frontiers of Germany proper, and half '*Auslandsdeutsche*', men of German ethnic origin from other countries; these included Alsace-Lorraine, Bessarabia, Croatia, Poland, the Sudetenland and Slovakia.

Among these were:

Oberscharführer (Staff-Sergeant)	— Georg Gerk	— in charge of the Camp garage

	Götze — who later replaced Högelow Kehrer — in charge of the Quartermasters' Stores Krellmann — a medical orderly
Scharführer Sergeant)	— Lindenau — from Hamburg; Guard Commander
Unterscharführer (Corporal)	— Gessner — from Stettin; in charge of Canteen formerly in Oranienburg. Kranenbröcker — a senior Party member; an NCO of the Guard Georg Rebs — A French army deserter; an NCO in charge of hut Willi Römer — Guard Commander Wese — former Czech army NCO; reported to have shot the German political prisoner Rudi Busch, who had been a prisoner for 11 years. Witwer — in charge of a construction squad
Rottenführer (Lance Corporal)	— Paulsen — as NCO in charge of a hut Otto Suckut — from Western Poland
Sturmmann (Junior Private)	— Figge — from Worms; medical orderly during withdrawal from Alderney Klingenberg — from Danzig Kuhlmann — later promoted to officer rank Neumann — from Stettin; in charge of guard dogs Philips — from Emsland; in charge of a construction squad
SS-Mann (Private)	— Bittenbinder — from Bessarabia Ernst — from Croatia Klaus — from Croatia Kristian — in charge of construction squad Popp — from Croatia Rometsch — from Croatia; reported to have shot the Czech prisoner Josef Lammel Wolf — from Croatia

List's immediate superior was in Germany and he did not come under local jurisdiction. He admitted or refused to admit whom he chose. He drew his rations and other stores in bulk from the Army on indent at normal prescribed scales, but was not thereafter accountable to the Army for them. The camp had its own independent quarter-masters stores, and ran its own kitchen and canteen; the NCOs in charge of both the latter withheld food and prisoners' Red Cross parcels which they sold in France. The camp had its own transport and ran its own garage and workshop, the foundations of which can still be seen adjoining the cliff road. 'Trusty' prisoners were selected to assist in the administration of the camp, for example to wait on the SS staff and to run the SS canteen. Only a German prisoner might become a 'trusty'.

Operational deployment

The purpose behind the transfer of the Construction Brigade to Alderney was to provide additional manpower to help the OT with its construction programme for priority defence works. It was agreed between the Army Engineers, OT Operations Group West and the SS Command in France that despite the independence of the Brigade in matters of discipline, administration and economy, the operational deployment of the prisoners would be under the direction of the OT *Bauleiter*. Thus, when the *Bauleiter* had requirements placed on him by the Fortress Engineers, he was entitled to demand the required skilled or unskilled labour from the Brigade as available. Escorting the prisoners to and from work, and guarding them on the work site, remained the responsibility of the SS. The OT supervisors and foremen were only allowed to direct their work in technical matters, and all other communication with the prisoners was forbidden by the SS.

OT *Bauleiter* Ackermann and SS *Hauptsturmführer* List were both jealous of their rights as they saw them. Ackermann was senior in rank and charged with the direction of the whole labour force, including the Brigade, as might be technically most effective — as no doubt his engineering qualifications best fitted him to do. List was the proud senior representative of an élite corps, a key executive arm of a repressive, authoritarian regime, used to the exercise of arbitrary power. The two were bound to be incompatible. Ackermann, not a notorious sentimentalist when it came to his own bedraggled, half-starved, brutalised OT work force, was moved to make repeated oral complaints both to the Island Commandant, Zuske, and to the SS direct about the way they beat their prisoners on 'his' (Ackermann's) work sites, 'so that their capacity for work might be adversely affected'. This proprietorial tone may be a clue to Ackermann's motivation. He then protested in writing to Fortress Engineer Staff, who referred the protest back to the SS. One of the beaten prisoners had been a Jew, and so Ackermann now found himself the object of a counter-complaint by the SS that he was soft on Jews. He had the good fortune to have this firmly resisted by the senior OT engineer in the Cherbourg *Oberbauleitung* and the matter was not proceeded with; had it been, Ackermann might well have found himself on the wrong side of the wire at Sylt Camp or elsewhere.

There was a further bone of contention between Ackermann and List. Ackermann's immediate predecessor as *Bauleiter*, Dr Panzer, had been given written authority by the OT to punish recurrent offenders among his forced labour with up to 3 weeks' corrective imprisonment. As there was no normal German penal establishment on Alderney where these sentences might be served, it was agreed between superior OT and SS authorities that the Brigade might take such prisoners for up to 3 months. The OT *Frontführer, Haupttruppführer* Theo Konnertz, to whom Dr Panzer had delegated his power of detention, committed some 60 forced labourers to the concentration camp in this way between May and August 1943. But at the end of their sentences, the SS would not release them. After some effort on Ackermann's part, they were all ultimately returned to the OT in December 1943, some having in the meantime served as much as 8 months on a 3 months' sentence.

Ackermann won an apparent victory in late 1943 when the OT *Oberbauleitung* in Cherbourg negotiated the evacuation of the prisoners from Sylt Camp on 20 December. But they only went as far as Cherbourg where some half of them were given conditional release and mobilised into the Armed Forces (a not unusual proceeding at this stage of the war). The remainder, now only some 500 strong, were returned to Alderney in January 1944. However, the direct relationship between Ackermann and the prisoners detailed to his construction sites was not resumed. Overall technical control on the sites passed from him to the Fortress Engineers of the Army.

Conditions of Work

The inmates of the concentration camp were, of course, state prisoners, whether as criminals convicted before a normal court of law or as political prisoners under the administrative provisions of the regime. They therefore had no civil rights, wore the striped pyjama-like uniform, and were known not by name but by number displayed prominently on the back of their blouse. Each wore a coloured patch to show at a glance the category of offence for which he was being held; red for political, pink for homosexual, green for habitual criminal, purple for conscientious objector, and so on. Russian prisoners of war carried the letters 'SU' in red.

The hours of work on the outside sites were the same as for the OT labour force. Sometimes the prisoners were given exceptionally hard work to perform, as for example the four squads each of about 40 men who were attached to Fortress Cable Platoon (*Festungskabelzug*) I/1. The prescribed quota per man per day was a length of cable trench 5 metres long, 2.20 metres deep and half a metre wide, in rocky soil. Yet in spite of the condition both of the ground and the weakened prisoners, the officer commanding that platoon continually pressed for a further increase in the pace of work; indeed he boasted that he had multiplied the effort of the prisoners five-fold since he took over from his predecessor.

The theoretical scale of rations was also the same: Scale II for the SS staff and the special scale between III and IV for the prisoners. Only as with the OT this is not what the individual actually received to eat. The same problems of undernourishment occurred, and the same desperate, individual attempts to relieve it. This situation was compounded in the concentration camp by the diversion of part of the prisoners' rations to the SS canteen, where they were sold to the staff as extras. The profits from this were such that after two or three months each of the 100 odd SS staff received a 100 *Reichsmark* dividend from the canteen fund.

Medical facilities for the prisoners in the concentration camp were nominal. There was no German doctor and the sick bay was not properly equipped. An attempt by a visiting Air Force medical officer to supply drugs and anaesthetics was refused by the SS. The medical examination of prisoners and such treatment as was possible was carried out by prisoner doctors, one of whom was a dermatologist and another an ear specialist. Death certificates had to be signed by one of the German medical officers on the Island, but they were not normally allowed to see the bodies and the cause of death was already on the form they were required to sign. Some medical officers refused certificates on those terms; one justified the system by saying there were no proper facilities for post mortems, so there was no point in his seeing the bodies.

Discipline and brutality

The internal discipline at the lower echelon was maintained by prisoners themselves. In return for perquisites which eased the rigour of their confinement, selected prisoners were given authority to punish their fellows, provided they did so with sufficient brutality to satisfy those who gave them that authority — and who took it away if they did not. The immediate superior of each hut or working squad, known as the 'Kapo', thus had a vested interest, supported by higher authority, in making the lot of his particular group more harsh in return for personal relief. Even Ackermann, hostile to the SS, remarked with amazement how well the Kapos were treated where 'every Kapo had a room to himself with a soft bed and white linen'. Small wonder that Kapos did not want to jeopardise their preferment. As one of the German crane operators at the harbour said on observing a beating: 'One of the Kapos told me: "If I do not do it, I will get it in the evening myself".' The guards often only needed to begin where the prisoner foremen left off. An Able Seaman from MAA 605 described a camp beating:

'Shortly before my birthday on 25 May 1943, I visited the canteen at the Sylt concentration camp in an endeavour to buy some cognac. Nobody was allowed to enter the inner compound, but I had no difficulty in entering the outer compound. The canteen was run by German prisoners, 'trusties'. Whilst I was in the outer compound, I saw four men from the inner compound being escorted to the gate between the two compounds. One of them was weeping bitterly and was kicked and pushed about accordingly by the escort who called the sentry. An SS corporal came out and took the prisoners. The escort went away. Then the SS corporal called two SS men from the guardroom and went into the guardroom himself to get a whip. The handle of this whip was made of inter-woven leather thongs, the whole whip was made of leather. I saw the whip later in the outer guardroom and recognised it. From the canteen I could see the corporal indicating to the SS men that they were to fasten the four prisoners to the barbed wire with handcuffs, their hands above their heads. Their feet remained unfettered. After the prisoners had been handcuffed to the gate, they were whipped by the corporal, not one after the other but at random. One man was bent double with pain and raised his feet from the ground so that he was hanging by his arms. From where I was I could hear their cries of anguish somewhat dulled. This whipping, carried out by the corporal in the presence of the two guards, lasted ten minutes. The prisoner who had wept on his arrival was unable to walk properly when they were let free. As he staggered, he was pushed after the others towards the middle of the compound, where I lost sight of him. All four prisoners were Russians and wore the red flash. When I asked the prisoner working in the canteen why the men had been punished in this manner, he explained that these prisoners had taken a lamb, killed it and eaten it. The Russians did this owing to their hunger. At the slaughterhouse I often saw the Russians taking the bloody entrails surreptitiously from the bins.'

The compound gate seems to have been a favourite place. One of the SS guards recorded:

'In spring 1944, a German convict who had absented himself from his working site was recaptured and bound to the camp gate. His hands were crossed behind his back and bound

together and in this most painful manner the man was held up
bound to the gate for several hours.'

Escape — but to where, you may ask? — was a constant problem in the
eyes of the keepers, though for the most part prisoners only sought the
prospect of getting enough food to sustain life in their rigorous
circumstances by going absent for long enough to beg or steal
something to eat. A corporal of 319 divisional transport, who spent
three years in Alderney and was working in the ration office in the
Court House in New Street, told with some feeling how he witnessed
the recapture of a demoted ex-Kapo named Ebert who escaped from
the concentration camp in summer 1943:

'It was made known by a telephone call to all units that this man
Ebert had escaped from Sylt Camp. He spoke several languages
and may have hoped to get away on one of the transport ships
visiting Alderney. The whole Island was searched, and in the end
it turned out that he had sought refuge in the church between
Victoria Street and New Street. A Kapo climbed on to the roof,
smashed a window and opened the door, the SS men entered the
church and Ebert was led out. They beat him with iron bars, but
still he tried to run away, hoping the SS would not shoot for fear
of hitting their comrades who were standing in a row along his
way. He ran through the graveyard towards New Street, but
before he reached the street the SS fired and hit him three times. I
came out of my office, which was immediately opposite, in time
to see *Hauptmann* (Captain) Söchtling arrive in his car. Ebert ran
towards him, bleeding from the side of his head, his chest and his
thigh, and implored him to save him. He kept repeating: "*Herr
Hauptmann*, please help me, they are going to kill me." But
Hauptmann Söchtling made a gesture with his hand to keep him
away and said: "Go away: I do not want to have anything to do
with you", and went into his house which was opposite the Court
House. Ebert tried to hold on on my side of the road by seizing the
concrete pillars in front of our building and holding on to the
iron gate, but the SS men kicked his hands away and trod into his
stomach with their boots, so that he slumped forward, and when
he fell they shot him in the body. He was dying and asked for
some water, whereupon one of the SS men kicked him on the
head. He died then shortly afterwards, just in front of our
windows, after one of the SS men had finished him off with a shot
in the head. There was some argument about this afterwards
between the SS men, as some had wanted to bring him back to
the camp alive for interrogation. A soldier from the Signals Unit
was accidentally wounded during the shooting in the churchyard.'

There have been persistent rumours, all of which seem to have originated after the war, that there were mass killings in the concentration camps, with hundreds of bodies being thrown over the cliff. The known figures for prisoners evacuated in 1943 and 1944 suggest that the number of those who were killed was relatively small. The suffering of the inmates is well-documented, but this was no 'death camp', no Auschwitz. Moreover, in a crowded, closed community like the German garrison on Alderney it will have been difficult to do anything, especially outside the camp, without it being seen, generally known among the Germans (though not necessarily to the relatively few employed Channel Island workers, who were not as a rule in very close touch) and by May 1945 freely talked about by soldiers who showed themselves only too willing to demonstrate criticism of their fellow-countrymen's inhuman behaviour, particularly on the part of the SS. It is also noteworthy that the surviving forced labourers in the Channel Islands did not substantiate these rumours when questioned in 1945 when memories were fresh.

Departure

The SS *Baubrigade* I left Sylt Camp and it was closed in June 1944. The camp was then destroyed and used by the Armed Forces as construction material elsewhere and for firewood.

It may have been as well for the prisoners that this was so, for on 10 May 1944 the Island Commandant, by then Lieutenant-Colonel Schwalm, issued a written order, classified 'Secret' and 'Not to fall into enemy hands', which read:

> '*Safe custody of Concentration Camp Prisoners. (Sylt Camp)*
> On receipt of the second degree of alarm, the concentration camp prisoners will be immediately collected in Sylt Camp and kept under the strictest supervision by SS guard personnel. Attempts at breakout or escape will be rendered impossible. In no circumstances will prisoners be allowed to fall into the hands of the enemy. For the rest, the Camp Commandant will act in accordance with instructions received by him from *Reichsführer SS*.'

Extract from the log book of the 'Gerfried':

> 'Voyage Alderney-Guernsey-Jersey-St Malo between 24 May and 1 June 1944

24 June 1944	2300 Alderney	280 prisoners taken aboard
25 June 1944	0240 left Alderney	
25 June 1944	0710 Guernsey	prisoners unloaded
27 June 1944	2100 Guernsey	prisoners reloaded
27 June 1944	2300 left Guernsey	

28 June 1944	0340 Jersey	prisoners unloaded
29 June 1944	2300 Jersey	prisoners reloaded
30 June 1944	0220 Jersey	prisoners unloaded again
30 June 1944	2100 Jersey	prisoners reloaded again
30 June 1944	2315 left Jersey	
1 July 1944	0950 St Malo	prisoners unloaded'

Note by the Master of the 'Gerfried', Captain Krönke:

'The prisoners were in the hold which has a deck area of 90 square metres and a volume of 270 cubic metres'.

As one of the SS guards put it:

'Braun gave the order that all the men were to be loaded and crammed into the hold like sardines in a tin'.

The rest of the prisoners were transported on board the 'Schwalbe' whose Master, Captain Kröger, was noted for a less sympathetic attitude towards the prisoners' suffering than that of Captain Krönke.

On arrival in St Malo, the prisoners and their guards travelled for over five weeks by train across France and Belgium to Kortemark, where they had further construction tasks to perform on V1 sites. They eventually returned to Germany, having been renamed SS *Baubrigade* 5, destination Buchenwald.

In Belgium the train was on a number of occasions attacked by the RAF, and in the confusion a number of the prisoners escaped. Arising from this incident comes one of those extraordinary happenings which are sometimes brought about by extreme circumstances; to it we owe our first detailed account of Sylt Camp while Alderney was still occupied, and it provides a happy postscript to this unhappy chapter.

It concerns a Czech and a Slovak — in case either or both of them returned home after the war it might be a kindness not to name them, to avoid any current embarrassment to them. The Czech was a political prisoner who had been arrested by the Germans soon after the occupation of Bohemia and had been held — without trial, of course — in a succession of concentration camps. The Slovak was an SS man.

The differences between them were as great as can be envisaged, apart from their ability to understand each other's speech. The Czech was a literate, sophisticated, politically-minded social-democrat. The Slovak was a semi-literate primitive. Czechs and Slovaks have in the past, despite Dr Masaryk's political achievement in 1919, not always been willing partners and friends. In the early 1940s, this historical antipathy was intensified: the Czechs were a subject people held down by the Third Reich under occupation as the Protectorate of Bohemia and Moravia; the Slovaks had an independent republic which was allied to Hitler as what we would now call a satellite state. The Czech was, therefore, from the Third Reich's point of view, an enemy of the people being held, without rights, so that he might do no political damage. The Slovak was an ally, allowed to join the élite force guarding the Czech.

They met in SS *Baubrigade* 1 in Alderney, one on each side of the wire. And the impossible happened: they became friends.

No doubt the Czech could do with a helping hand outside, and no doubt the Slovak saw the war going badly and needed a reinsurance policy, but the relationship between these two men — and it was not homosexual — was more than this, as was discovered in the fulness of time. The pair had planned to escape together at a suitable moment that would take them into Allied protection, and this moment came in Belgium in August 1944. They made their way to Allied lines and became, at any rate for the moment, prisoners of war.

But were they? The Czech was not a prisoner of war but a liberated ally; he would present no problem if released and handed to the Czechoslovak authorities in exile, who would no doubt induct him into the Czechoslovak forces in Britain. The Slovak presented no problem as a prisoner of war who had been serving with the Germans, but if he were handed to the Czechoslovak authorities he might well be shot as a traitor or condemned as a war criminal from the SS *Totenkopfverband.*

As far as the two men themselves were concerned, they had come this far together at the risk of their lives and did not wish to part company at any price; indeed the Czech was prepared to stay interned as a prisoner of war for the privilege.

But the administration could naturally only see that one was a prisoner of war and the other was not, so whatever their own feelings in the matter they must be separated. However, at this stage some hitch in the proceedings seemed to occur and they remained together for some time classed as 'in transit' — hopefully until some more sensible solution was found.

CHAPTER SIX

The Odds and....

THE RISE in numbers in both garrison and work force in Alderney from the end of 1941 onwards inevitably meant more headquarter elements to direct them and more administering services to sustain them. We have seen the expansion in the fighting arms in Chapter Four. Let us now consider the headquarters, the ancilliary units and some of the camp followers.

Headquarters

The main Headquarters of the Island Commandant (*Inselkommandantur*) — later known as the Fortress HQ (*Festungskommandantur*) — was at Seymour House in Connaught Square. This was the Island Commandant's administrative office. The staff were billeted in Victoria Street and New Street and fed from a communal kitchen in High Street. The Island Commandant also had a tactical or operational HQ (*Gefechtsstand*), from which command was to be exercised over fighting units on the Island should they be actively deployed in the field. This operational HQ was in a 30-foot, 4-storey tower built for the purpose (now destroyed) on the north side of the Longis Road on the outskirts of St Anne. It was known to the troops as the *Hoffmannshöhe*, abbreviated to *Ho-höhe*, after Captain Carl Hoffmann, the first operational Island Commandant.

We have seen how Hoffmann was followed by Gleden and Rohde and then, from February 1942 by Major (later Lieutenant-Colonel) Zuske. Zuske was succeeded on 1 November 1943 by Major (later Lieutenant-Colonel) Schwalm, hitherto commanding officer of the I Battalion of Grenadier Regiment 582 in Jersey. Schwalm retained his post as Island Commandant until the end of the war.

Thus all Island Commandants were Army officers. This was not because in the German Armed Services the Army was the Senior Service — after all, Vice-Admiral Hüffmeier held overall command in the Channel Islands in the last days of the war — but rather because the majority of fighting troops that would need tactical command if engaged in active operations were Army units.

Schwalm moved his billet to Longis House, which he shared with the Senior Naval Officer.

The Navy's operational command of its units was exercised from a

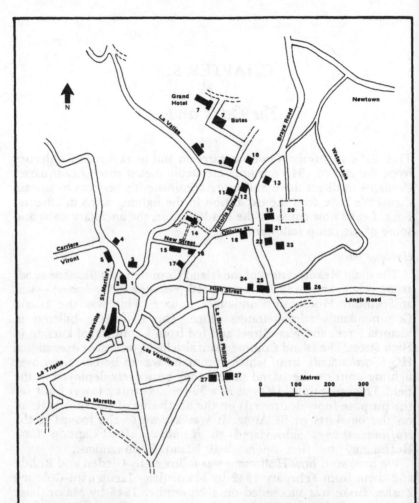

1. Connaught Square
2. Island Commandant's HQ
3. Soldatenheim
4. Observation tower
5. Mouriaux House
6. Moroccan PW billets
7. Flak HQ and workshops
   (Grand Hotel and Butes Arsenal)
8. Bakery
9. Food store (Methodist Chapel)
10. Petrol dump
11. Military Hospital
12. Communal kitchen
13. Val des Portes mess
14. Parish Church and churchyard
15. Court House building
16. Pay Office
17. Out-station HQ of FK 515
18. Billeting office and store
    (Militia Arsenal)
19. Slaughterhouse
20. Underground storage dump
21. Coal dump
22. Carpenter's shop
23. Furniture store
24. Military police (Jubilee Home)
25. Cinema
26. "Hoffmannshöhe" — tactical HQ
27. Naval operational HQ and
    communications centre

The Town

separate tactical headquarters (*Gefechtsstand*) in a wooden hut erected in 1943 on the west side of the southern extension of the Brecque Philippe. The administrative offices were in the Harbour Commandant's office.

In the absence of the airfield, which, as we have seen, was not operational throughout the war, the Air Force was effectively represented by the anti-aircraft artillery on the Island. *Flak* HQ, commanding these units, was in the Grand Hotel, which housed both offices and some of the staff, the remainder being billeted in nearby houses. Their transport, workshop and armourer's shop were in adjoining outbuildings and the small Arsenal on the Butes opposite.

The civil administration, such as it was without a civilian population, was conducted by the Outstation of *Feldkommandantur* 515 — renamed *Platzkommandantur* early in 1944 — in Lloyds Bank in Victoria Street. *Sonderführer* Herzog was replaced in April 1942 by *Militärverwaltungsoberinspektor* Hans Spann until March 1944 when he was relieved in turn by *Sonderführer* Wilhelm Richter.

Communications

The split in command between the three armed services was reflected in the communication channels. Each service had its separate telephone exchange, connected to the parent formation in Guernsey or Jersey. Each unit and sub-unit was connected to its appropriate service exchange on the Island. As the three exchanges were interconnected, so that calls could be cross-routed, the system was not as tiresome in practice as it sounds in theory, and worked quite efficiently. And key locations, like Fort Albert, for example, had lines to all three exchanges.

The Army signals centre, operated by the signals staff of Channel Islands Command (*Heeresnachrichtenzug Kanalinseln*) was based in the old civilian post office in Victoria Street, with a teleprinter outstation at the top of the Venelles. A naval signals office was situated in the cellar of the Harbour Commandant's office, but the main naval telephone exchange was at the top of the Brecque Philippe, adjoining naval tactical HQ. The Air Force signals office and telephone exchange was on the Longis Road, almost opposite the Island Commandant's tactical HQ — the *Ho-höhe*.

There was a lamp signalling station on top of Fort Albert and a wireless station at the top of the Trigale on the north side.

Administration

From August 1942, an officer known as the Garrison Officer (*Garnisonsoffizier*) was made responsible overall for billeting, electricity, water, sewage and waste disposal on behalf of the whole garrison.

One of the less exciting but essential offices of the military administrative apparatus under the Garrison Officer was the Army Billeting Office (*Heeresunterkunftsverwaltung* — HUV). The HUV in Alderney was an outstation of its parent HUV in St Lô in Normandy. It was responsible for the maintenance, furnishing and allocation of quarters both for the German garrison and for those civilians directly employed by them. As such it was responsible to the Garrison Officer for all the Island property used as housing. This included perhaps half the houses in St Anne, particularly in the central area, most of the houses down the Longis Road, Braye Road, Braye Street, Whitegates, Simon's Place, Coastguards, the Nunnery and a number of outlying properties convenient for more remote gun crews, like the bungalow above Fort Tourgis, on which the local Flak troop mounted a searchlight and in which the troop commander lived, and 'Quatre Vents', which accommodated the crew of the radar on the cliffs facing Coque Lihou. All the forts were occupied by troops except Platte Saline and Corblets, known to the Germans as '*Strandfeste*', Beach Fort. The HUV operated stores for furniture and fittings in the old Militia Arsenal in Ollivier Street and in two wooden huts in the fields to the east of the Val, above the house which served as their carpenters' shop. The HUV also ran the mess at Val des Portes, known to the troops as '*Das Generalshaus*', which was strictly intended for important visitors but inhabited for a time by Carl Hoffmann and more permanently by the Senior Engineer Officer.

In general, all billets were provided with concrete underground air-raid shelters.

The civilian employees, who worked mainly for HUV, in the canteens or on the farms, were a mixed bag of Channel Islanders, Irishmen and British from the other islands, over 100 at peak. They worked as carpenters, glaziers, bricklayers, plasterers, drivers, cooks and waitresses, on drainage work, on the farms, in the electricity works and the canteens, and as fishermen. They were mostly billeted in St Anne and fed in their billets from a communal kitchen in the Victoria Hotel to a ration scale slightly below that of the Armed Forces — which they did, in fact, receive. They were paid, had access to canteen shops and generally led as normal a life as the circumstances permitted. They thus constituted a more privileged group quite distinct from the main labour force in the camps that worked on construction sites.

One of the most peculiar anomalies among all the nationalities on Alderney in the course of the war were the Moroccan prisoners of war, taken from the French Army after the capitulation of 1940, who were billeted on the east side of Hauteville and in the Mare Jean Bott. There were also 100 Italian prisoners of war, in uniform, employed on general fatigue duties and quartered in Norderney camp.

All food supplies in the Island were centrally administered by the Army. Reference has already been made to ration scales and the bulk issues to the labour and concentration camps. The Army Ration Office (*Heeresverpflegungsamt* — HVA) had its office and central store in the Court House in New Street and its staff were billeted in Victoria Street. It had a number of subsidiary stores, notably for a time the Parish Church (flour, tinned goods and wine), the Salvation Army Hall (flour) and the Methodist Church (potatoes). The Roman Catholic Church, then at Crabby, was an OT sub-depot.

Meat supplies were handled by the slaughterhouse — a new slaughterhouse was built on the site of the present States Dairy in the Val. Bread was provided by a field bakery which operated first from Odoire's bakehouse in the Mare Jean Bott and then, in 1943, moved to new and enlarged custom-built premises in the Vallée, staffed by a team of 15 army bakers sent specially from Granville. There was also an auxiliary bakery at Fort Albert.

Medical facilities — or the lack of them — have been mentioned as they affected the labour force. For the garrison the situation was satisfactory and normal according to field provisions. Each major group — the Navy, the Air Force, the Army Engineers, the OT etc — ran its own Medical Inspection Room. The Mignot Memorial Hospital, then at the bottom of Victoria Street, was the MI room for the garrison battalion and also Military Hospital for all members of the Armed Forces unless their illness was so severe as to warrant evacuation. Civilian employees (as defined earlier in this chapter, not the labour force on construction work) were at first given medical attention by the OT doctor, but this was found so unsatisfactory and led to so much complaint that the Army doctors agreed to accept them at the garrison MI Room. All emergency surgical cases, for all arms of the service, civilian workers and OT personnel, were handled at the Military Hospital. There was a resident Army Dental Officer with a surgery in Victoria Street, opposite the Hospital.

A number of Casualty Reception Stations were prepared for use in the event of military action in the Island. The most sophisticated of these, CRS for the Central Sector (*Truppenverbandplatz Mitte*), was the underground concrete bunker still to be seen on the south side of the Longis Road near Longis House. It had a capacity of 25 beds and was well equipped, including an operating theatre.

Most units or sub-units maintained their own vehicle parks at some convenient nearby location: the Island Commandant's in St Martins behind the HQ building, the Flak behind the Grand Hotel and at the bottom of the Water Lane, the Navy at the top of the Venelles near their tactical HQ, FK 515 near their main farm complex, and so on. One platoon of 319 Infantry Division's divisional transport park was stationed in Alderney. In addition the Army had a maintenance workshop and paint shop in St Martins. There was also a horse-drawn transport sub-unit, the 13th Administrative Company (*Wirtschaftskompagnie*).

Two transport groups deserve special mention. Reference has been made to civilian drivers employed by the Billeting Office. These drivers were accommodated in Mouriaux House and kept their vehicles in the stables behind. There was also a squadron of trucks at the disposal of the OT, run by the National Socialist Transport Corps (*Nationalsozialistisches Kraftfahrerkorps* — NSKK), another para-military organisation of the Party which played an auxiliary role where required. Their vehicle park was at the bottom of the road leading up to Essex Castle, and their billets on the seaward side of that road, overlooking Longis Bay, were a happy hunting ground for some of the female civilian employees.

The Island Pay Office (*Inselzahlmeisterei*) was situated at the east end of New Street.

Law and Order

In general the maintenance of law and order within the garrison and among civilian employees was a responsiblity of FK 515. They had under command one section of the 319 divisional military police (*Feldgendarmerie*) consisting of one officer, three warrant officers and four NCOs. They were billeted in Connaught Square but operated from the Jubilee Old People's Home in the High Street. They policed the Island, maintained a strict black-out after dark and for a time administered the lock-up at the Court House. This was used both for military defaulters and for delinquent civilian employees on whom the Military Court was given authority to pass sentences of up to three months imprisonment; any more serious case had to be sent to Guernsey for trial. The officer in charge, Police Inspector (*Polizeiinspektor*) Sturm, was largely preoccupied with the higher aspects of police work at the *Feldkommandantur*, so that the day to day running of the section at the Jubilee Home was effectively left to one of the senior warrant officers (*Stabsfeldwebel*).

From 1943 onwards, the administration of the cells at the Court House lock-up and some additional emergency cell accommodation for military detainees passed to the Garrison Officer. These cells were used for all those with sentences of seven days or more in detention, with or without hard labour, where the case was not serious enough to warrant transfer out of the Island; they also accommodated soldiers on remand. Prisoners were usually housed three or more in one communal cell, so that a maximum of up to 60 could be accommodated, on average two thirds German military and one third civilians; they were never mixed.

Gaol conditions were unsatisfactory. Shortage of water for ablutions and sanitation was blamed by the Garrison Officer on the incapacity of the electricity supply to pump enough for the prison's requirements; but this difficulty does not seem to have affected other premises, the rest of the garrison washed and flushed satisfactorily, so the excuse sounds specious. The prisoners were blamed by the Garrison Officer for blocking up their own lavatories. Central heating was installed, but when it was switched off its value as an improvement on their previous stove heating must have seemed questionable to the inmates. The Garrison Officer's response to this charge — he was not a wit — sounds disingenuous:

> 'The inmates had two mattresses, four blankets and greatcoats, and some of them had their squad coats with which they used to cover themselves. Consequently nobody could really say he suffered from cold, particularly as I did not check whether the men undressed before they went to bed or not.'

With blocked lavatories and the statutory weekly bath only when the water pump was working well, it was by military standards an unhygienic mess. To add to the chaos, when the garrison rations were increased at the very end of the war, when it was seen that long term stocks would no longer be necessary, and the military prisoners' ration was correspondingly also increased, this was ruled to be 'an error by the kitchen staff' and the ration was promptly reduced from 700 grammes of bread per day back to 300.

Agriculture

Reference has already been made to the early farming activities started by the Out-Station of FK 515 under *Sonderführer* Herzog. In late 1942, direction of farming passed from FK 515 to the OT and was supervised from January 1943 by *Obertruppführer* Rebling. By that summer, Herzog's first pioneering efforts had been developed into quite a lively industry in spite of mismanagement through incompetence; in fairness to OT one should perhaps say that they had come to Alderney to build concrete works, not till the ground or rear sheep.

There were four main sites:

> The 'Island Farm' (*Inselfarm*, also known as *Gutshof*), built by the Germans behind the old brickfield, where Alderney Nurseries have now inherited the German building. This was the centre of agricultural activity. Mignot Farm, just off the Rose Farm road (Grand Val). Rose Farm, at the other end of the same east-west road. Mill Farm below the Bonne Terre.

They were run with the help of civilian employees, forced labourers and prisoners.

At the height of their development, they were growing barley, oats, potatoes and vegetables. The potato target for 1942 was 8,000 cwt and in fact 3,600 cwt were harvested. In 1943, despite complete failure in one seventh of the area planted, 250 tons were harvested. They raised pigs. They increased their sheep flock from 30 in 1942 to over 300 by late summer 1943, and had a successful lambing season that spring. They kept a herd of cows for both milk and beef, but some of the cows were diseased so that those drinking the milk blamed it for the worms they developed under their skin.

The farms reverted to control by FK 515 in July 1944, by which time *Sonderführer* Richter was in charge.

In addition to these larger agricultural undertakings, many individuals grew vegetables in the gardens of their billets in order to augment their diet. A part of Vallée Gardens was used by the main Army canteen in the same way.

At the beginning of the occupation, it had been the intention that Alderney should produce foodstuffs for the larger garrison on Guernsey. But as the war progressed and the Alderney garrison multiplied, this plan was overtaken by events and all food produced was consumed on the Island. From summer 1944 onwards they concentrated on milk as they found themselves under siege.

Supply

In normal circumstances, the three essential supply commodities for modern forces at war are food, ammunition and what the British Army in its wisdom called 'Petrol, Oil and Lubricants'. In the case of Alderney as the war dragged on into siege, the second two became less important as there was little expenditure of stocks on campaigning, and the first became all-important after the re-occupation of neighbouring French areas by the Allies in summer 1944.

The German Armed Forces had quite early on realised the need for the Island to carry large stocks of essentials to enable it to withstand siege or sustained assault. It was laid down that Alderney should maintain a reserve of 90 days' iron rations for the garrison's use in emergency. Accordingly the Germans constructed central dumps and also a number of small, decentralised storage points for the immediate local supply of outlying positions.

The largest dump, storing food, ammunition and petrol, consisted of tunnels hollowed out from the hillside beside the Water Lane, beneath where Auderville now stands, east of the upper Braye Road. It had several entrances, some of them big enough for trucks to drive in, one as much as 14 feet high. Another was dug into the hillside just above Fort Tourgis, on the other (east) side of the road. Smaller dumps for ammunition storage were in the small quarry at the foot of the hill below Essex Castle, on both the north and south sides of the Longis Road, and in the hillside south of Longis Villas. These were all under permanent guard. Two small ammunition storage tunnels were also dug in the low rock cliff at the north-east and south-east corners of the New Harbour.

Two emergency stocks of petrol were established: some 300 drums each of 200 litres were stored in a hut just south of the Butes, beside what is now Butes Lodge Hotel; 50,000 litres in 200 litre drums were stacked in the open at the approach to the Little Blaye, just west of Carrière Viront. Both were under permanent guard.

It should not be forgotten that under the rubric 'Food' must be included that essential, water. The garrison alone was about double the pre-war civilian population, who had enjoyed no mains water; and on top of the garrison, there was the labour force. So the largest population Alderney has ever seen faced a problem.

The Germans solved it piecemeal, partly for reasons of engineering convenience, but largely because a variety of water sources and distribution channels was less vulnerable to enemy attack or sabotage.

The principal reservoir was a concrete bunker at the corner of the Rose Farm Road and what is now Allée ès Fées, which at any rate for part of the time was equipped with some chlorination facility of doubtful efficacy. It was fed from the springs at Rose Farm and at the bottom of the approach road to the airport, and also from a pumping station in the Water Lane. The site was selected because it was on high ground so that supply could be by gravity, which carried the water by pipe to the more important buildings in Connaught Square, to stand-pipes at the Grand Hotel, the hospital, the slaughterhouse and Newtown, and also supplied some houses at Braye and the Harbour Commandant's office. Units in this whole area were supplied by tank-wagon from these distribution points.

Outlying supply channels were: from the spring near Essex House by pump to a storage tank at Essex Castle and thence by gravity feed to all troops in the eastern part of the Island; from the spring at Haize to a storage tank raised on pillars on the higher ground south of Borkum Camp, supplying that camp, Blücher and Falke batteries, and units in the central sector; from the spring in Trois Vaux to a storage tank at the *Westbatterie*, supplying that battery, other troops on the Giffoine, and Sylt Camp; from Mannez Quarry beside Corblets Bay to a storage tank above Saye Farm for the garrison at Château à l'Etoc, Norderney Camp and for onward pumping to Fort Albert; from the stream in the Petit Val to a storage tank on the hillside above Helgoland Camp for that camp only; and from the Bonne Terre at Bridge of Martin for the troops in Fort Tourgis only.

The generation and distribution of electricity was similarly on a piecemeal basis, though gridded together. The Germans ran five generating stations, each supplying its own surrounding area in the first instance, but available to reinforce others through the grid. These generators were at the pre-war electricity works at the Hèche, at the bottom of the Water Lane, at Crabby — opposite the present electricity works — at the Arsenal below Fort Albert and at the *Westbatterie*. A variety of generating equipment was used, British, Belgian and German, all of it driven by diesel except for the Water Lane plant which was served by steam. This latter had to be fuelled with coal or wood which presented problems as oil is more easily transportable. Electricity was thus supplied to virtually all units at 220 volts or 380 volts on 3 phases by overhead wiring, largely of aluminium. Fittings were shipped in from France.

In addition, each unit had an emergency stock of carbide lamps, fuel for which was kept in a special store in (perhaps oddly) the OT dump.

There was a coal dump above the slaughterhouse in the Val, but the main coal depot consisted of anthracite type beans and bricquettes lying in the open at the top of Crabby Bay, below the Fort Grosnez glacis. In early 1944 this contained over 500 tons.

The OT ran a timber dump for their construction operations situated in the north-east quadrant of the crossroad Braye Road-Lower Road.

There was no gas and the pre-war gasworks were inoperative throughout the occupation.

The only quarry used for stone by the Germans was the Battery Quarry behind Braye Bay, where blasting at 1300 and 1800 hours was a regular feature at the height of the building season.

CHAPTER SEVEN

The Harbour

THE MAJORITY of the 600-odd naval personnel stationed in Alderney were marine artillery in coastal defence units. There were also marine infantry, whose role is described below. Although all these came under the control of OKM, the officers and men wore grey uniforms with marine artillery or infantry insignia, and not the usual navy blue. The 'Blue Navy' was represented only by the crews of the vessels based at Braye and by a relatively small staff responsible for the harbour there and for the Alderney end of shipping movements to and from the Island.

The Harbour Commandant (*Hafenkommandant*), who was also Naval Officer in Charge with overall responsibility for the naval contingent as a whole, was at first *Kapitänleutnant* (Lieutenant-Commander) Jacobi, under whom the treatment of Russian prisoners working in the harbour was probably at its worst; he was transferred in early 1943 first to Granville and then to Rouen. Then for a short time in mid-1943 *Fregattenkapitän* (Commander) Parsenow took over; there was a rumour that he was lost at sea during an action with the Royal Navy off Cap de la Hague. From August 1943 until the end of the war he was succeeded by *Korvettenkapitän* (Commander) Massmann, of whom we shall hear more anon.

Shore defence

The harbour's immediate approaches were covered by coastal defence guns, anti-aircraft guns, small arms and searchlights whose siting has already been referred to in Fort Albert, on Roselle Point, in Braye Bay and west of the breakwater at and near Forts Tourgis and Doyle. In the harbour itself were three further guns in concrete bunkers at Fort Grosnez, the largest of which had a 90° arc of fire and covered the whole outside (north-west side) of the breakwater.

Local defence was provided by machine gun and 2 cm AA gun posts in 'pill-boxes' on the eastern arm of the entry to the New Harbour (not always manned), a few yards further east to fire into the main harbour (always manned), in the eastern wall of the stone jetty — which the Germans had built out eastwards to straighten the angle and increase the quay area — and in an interesting two-tiered emplacement on the tip of the breakwater. This latter housed a 2 cm gun in a rotatable tank-

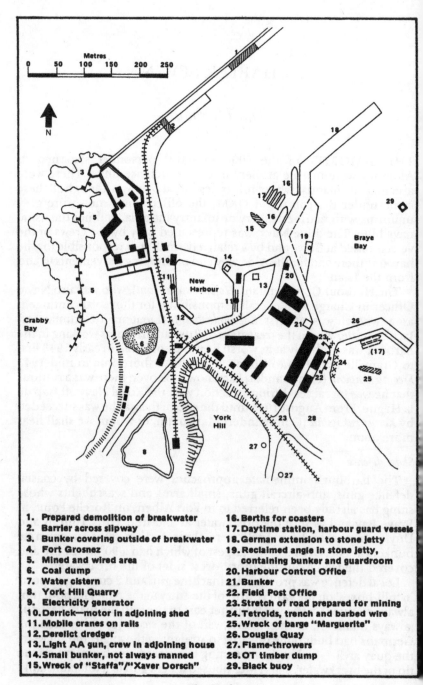

1. Prepared demolition of breakwater
2. Barrier across slipway
3. Bunker covering outside of breakwater
4. Fort Grosnez
5. Mined and wired area
6. Coal dump
7. Water cistern
8. York Hill Quarry
9. Electricity generator
10. Derrick—motor in adjoining shed
11. Mobile cranes on rails
12. Derelict dredger
13. Light AA gun, crew in adjoining house
14. Small bunker, not always manned
15. Wreck of "Staffa"/"Xaver Dorsch"
16. Berths for coasters
17. Daytime station, harbour guard vessels
18. German extension to stone jetty
19. Reclaimed angle in stone jetty, containing bunker and guardroom
20. Harbour Control Office
21. Bunker
22. Field Post Office
23. Stretch of road prepared for mining
24. Tetroids, trench and barbed wire
25. Wreck of barge "Marguerite"
26. Douglas Quay
27. Flame-throwers
28. OT timber dump
29. Black buoy

The Harbour

turret above a machine gun with a 180° traverse; some of the masonry
of the top walk of the breakwater had been demolished at its tip to
make this wide arc possible. At the bottom of Braye Street, where it
becomes the approach to the quay area, the Germans constructed a
bunker elaborately camouflaged as a house, with a false upper storey
built of wood, with blind, painted windows and a corrugated iron roof;
the field of fire of this bunker was eastwards across Braye Bay.

The landward approaches to the harbour were wired and mined.
The minefield in Braye Bay has already been described. Crabby Bay
between high water mark and the road was covered with a minefield
up to 30 yards across between barbed wire fences, and the road above
was prepared for demolition. The thinning extremity of this minefield
protruded northward along the rocks to the west of Grosnez Fort. The
base of the breakwater and slipway were cut by a barbed wire fence on
six-foot upright steel girders set in concrete. Sections of the breakwater
and the stone jetty were prepared for demolition. The approach to
Douglas Quay was guarded by a trench protected by tetroid obstacles.
Braye Street was prepared for mining, and the holes filled with wooden
plugs, as far southward as the flamethrowers at the bottom of the Braye
Road, so as to include the important north-south/east-west crossroad.

The harbour area was guarded by marine infantry under direct
command of the Harbour Commandant, working in three watches
each of six men by day, doubled at night. Their guardroom was in an
underground bunker at the base of the stone jetty, immediately
adjoining the emplacement built in the reclaimed area on its east side.
This Harbour Guard (*Hafenschutz*) was billeted in houses on the east
side of the Braye Road, upwards from the Harbour Commandant's
office which was in the bottom (most northerly) house. The Harbour
Guard controlled landward approaches to the harbour area, entry
being permitted in hours of darkness only by way of the main road
leading into the south end of Braye Street.

Sea defences

The entrance to the harbour was protected by a boom, the western
end of which was attached to the tip of the breakwater, the eastern end
to Bibette Head. In the middle was a narrow free passage or gate, the
western limit of which was marked by a large, square air-sea rescue
buoy. The two halves of the boom each consisted of a net suspended
from a top cable held up by small conical buoys strung at six eight foot
intervals, between large (six foot) floating cylinders. These latter were
anchored to the bottom by concrete blocks, as was also the large,
square buoy marking the gate. The gate was not normally closed.

By the beginning of 1944 the boom was in bad repair. The cable
fitted to the top of the conical buoys was described at that time by one
of the fishermen as 'sagging so far under water between each that a

boat drawing three feet can pass between the buoys'. A new boom was therefore prepared. This time the buoys were all six foot cylinders, brought by escort trawlers from Cherbourg and discharged straight on to the lower level of the breakwater. Here prisoners from the concentration camp assembled the new net and boom which was laid out along the length of the breakwater. The net was of circular chain mesh, each link of pencil-thick wire cable being about three inches in diameter.

The boom, once in use, was maintained and repaired on site by a French diver and his crew, operating from a dismantled French fishing boat without engine or mast, towed by the unarmed pilot-boat 'Lotse V'.

The remaining sea defence consisted of six harbour guard vessels (*Hafenschutzboote*). These were all 40-45 foot wooden French-type fishing boats, driven by diesel motors, with maximum speed of six knots. They were painted grey and carried two letters and a two-figured number on the bow. Each mounted forward one 2 cm AA gun, either single-barrelled or four-barrelled ('*Vierling*'), and was manned by a naval ('Blue Navy') crew of between eight and ten. Each also carried a wireless set and an inflatable rubber dinghy. They were normally berthed by day alongside each other outside any ships lying up against the western side of the stone jetty and in the Old Harbour.

At night two of these vessels took station just inside the boom, one by the square buoy west of the gate, and the other at the breakwater end. There was no regular patrolling round the Island by day or night as the power of the boats was insufficient to contend with the strong tides. They therefore spent most of their time in harbour. Occasionally one or more sailed in convoy to Cherbourg, but the only regular operational use to which they were put outside the harbour was to supply and relieve the Casquets lighthouse.

Lighthouses

There are two lighthouses in Alderney waters: Quesnard, at Mannez near the eastern tip of the Island; and Casquets, on an offshore rock six miles to the west. Both were used by the Germans during the occupation and manned by marine infantry under the Alderney Harbour Commandant.

The Casquets was at first manned by a crew of seven. They were all taken to England as prisoners of war during the Commando raid on 3 September 1942 — Operation 'Dryad'. The German lighthouse crew made their last signal to base in Cherbourg at 0020 on 3 September. Failure to make contact thereafter excited little concern because there had been repeated technical failures over the previous days and atmospheric disturbance was heavy. The Germans first discovered something was wrong when two of the harbour guard vessels based in

Alderney made a routine relief trip to Casquets on 4 September. No member of the lighthouse crew appeared to help unload stores, so a rubber dinghy with three men was sent over to the rock to investigate. They reported that lights were burning in all rooms and there were signs of hurried search; all seven of the crew were missing, the secret cupboard broken into, the radio destroyed and an external barbed wire obstacle laid on one side. The immediate finding was that the crew had been surprised and taken prisoner by a British raiding party and the discovery of a British woollen cap confirmed this. Senior Naval Officer Channel Islands (*Seekommandant Kanalinseln*), who happened to be visiting Alderney on that day, ordered the immediate re-occupation of the lighthouse by a relief crew of 11 petty officers and ratings from Alderney harbour.

Some argument then followed between the services as to whether the Casquets was the responsibility of the Navy as an aid to shipping or of 319 Infantry Division as a garrison of the occupied Channel Islands, or indeed, whether it needed to be manned at all. It was finally decided that the Navy should maintain a reinforced crew there, protected by 30 land mines, barbed wire and even three small flamethrowers; stricter security measures were to be observed. In the latter part of the war, the crew fluctuated between 20 and 30 marine infantrymen, armed with rifles and machine-pistols. For some months this group included a junior officer who volunteered to escape the consequences of an unfortunate *affaire* in France.

The Casquets was supplied by two of the harbour guard vessels about every ten days, weather permitting, and the men were rotated. The light at Casquets was not used in the latter part of the war, but the crew was still adjudged a valuable advanced observation post for Channel shipping and was furnished with a wireless transmitter and a heliograph to report its sightings to the *Westbatterie* on Alderney.

Quesnard lighthouse was used as a navigational aid for night convoys. The light would burn for up to two hours at a time, showing its normal flash pattern.

Marine traffic

Until the Allied invasion of Normandy in 1944, Alderney was supplied mainly by convoys from Cherbourg every ten days or so. A typical convoy consisted of five coasters of 300-400 tons, sailing under the German flag — although some of them were Dutch — and each armed with a single 2 cm AA gun on a raised platform aft. Each convoy was escorted by up to three armed trawlers, each mounting four-barrelled 2 cm AA guns on raised platforms forward and aft, a single 2 cm gun amidships and a small naval gun forward. All convoys sailed by night. The coasters had a normal turn-around time of three days while they discharged cargo. Once construction activity had tailed off, this consisted mainly of food, forage and cattle on the hoof for slaughtering. On the return trip they would carry any unwanted military stores, OT machinery and loads of scrap iron which had been retrieved from the dump in York Hill Quarry, just outside the harbour area.

Other traffic was irregular. The escort vessels often refused to carry civilian passengers (for example, French employees) to and from Cherbourg, in which case one of Alderney's harbour guard vessels would have to carry them, accompanying the next convoy out. Traffic between Alderney and the other islands was so erratic that on occasion it was found quicker to sail to Cherbourg, then travel overland to St Malo, and thence onward by more regular boat to Jersey or Guernsey. Rare convoys from Guernsey to Alderney sailed round Sark and up the Race, approaching Alderney harbour from the east, a trip of at least four hours. The western approach, the Swinge, was closed to coastal shipping.

Two black conical buoys marked the outer rocks at the east and west end of Braye Bay.

At the beginning of 1944 there was some experimentation with coloured flares fired by incoming vessels as recognition signals, but this does not seem to have been regularly adopted.

Apart from occasional brief visits from patrolling E-Boats, the harbour was not used operationally by other German naval craft. No U-Boats are known to have put in there.

The ships which finally evacuated the OT forced labourers and the concentration camp prisoners in summer 1944 were listed by the Naval Transport Officer as: 'Derfflinger', 'Franka', 'Gerfried', 'Holstein', 'Klaus Wilhelm', 'Lena', 'Spinel'.

Harbour working

The immediate operations of the harbour were controlled from an office in a hut at the base of the stone jetty, near the present entrance to the sailing club. It was manned by two marine infantrymen or naval ratings. In 1942, the Germans had completed a steel pier decked with wood as an extension to the original stone jetty, in order to accommodate the additional traffic required by the growing garrison and in particular to facilitate the unloading of the French barges bringing quantities of heavy stores for the construction of fortifications. Three five-ton cranes were fixed to this pier. Other loading facilities were a large static derrick at the north-west corner of the New Harbour, with a load of 20 tons; two mobile steam cranes on rails, one on each side of the New Harbour; and three five-ton mobile cranes mounted on caterpillar tracks, the property of the Hamburg firm Karl G. Blume. Dock labour was provided by prisoners from the concentration camp and forced labourers from the OT camps.

1. Coast Patrol (between Quesnard and Hommeaux Florains).

2. MAA 605 parading at Fort Albert.

3. Fort Quesnard.

4. *Westbatterie*: 15 cm. naval coastal artillery in concrete emplacemen (1945)

5. Giffoine: working party en route to the Westbatterie site.

6. One of the guns of *Batterie Elsass* at Fort Albert.

7. *Batterie Blücher*, Army coastal artillery.

8. Searchlight and machine gun at Château à l'Étoc.

9. Fort Albert: observation tower and rangefinder.

Mannez Hill: Fire
ntrol Tower (post-
r photograph).

Braye Bay: Beach Defences (1943?).

12. Bibette Head from Château à l'Étoc.

13. Minefield warning sign (1942).

14. Mouriaux: Observation Tower (post-war photograph showing addition of water tank at top).

15. Sylt Camp: View from the Commandant's châlet (post-war photograph on which originator has noted: 'Jersey was visible on the horizon to the naked eye').

Sylt Camp: the gate to the inner compound from the ruins of the SS Quarters, 1945.

'Star of David' cut by a Jewish forced labourer into the concrete shuttering of a ...ker.

18.   The Harbour from Fort Albert.

19.   Braye Harbour: Shipping alongside stone jetty (1941).

20.   The Harbour jetty.

21.   Braye: Rear of Braye Street: beach defences on right (1942).

22. Relieving the Casquets Lighthouse.

23. Quesnard Lighthouse.

24.   French OT employees: Original is captioned in German handwriting: '2 French auxiliary personnel for Org. Todt, Alderney'. (1942).

25.   Victoria Street.

as kann doch

einen Schwager

nicht erschüttern

26 & 27. Two of the few remaining murals in bunkers. The longer text reads: 'He kno no honours outwardly shown, only his hard duty. With earnest eye and pale cheek he goes quietly to his death. Late or early, he is simple and brave, undaunted in storm. Unpretentious infantry! May God protect you'.

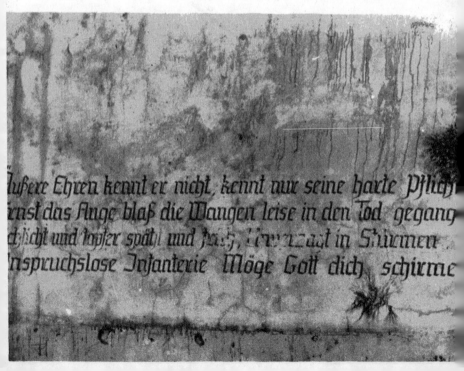

Äußere Ehren kennt er nicht, kennt nur seine harte Pflich
ernst das Auge blaß die Wangen leise in den Tod gegang
glich und tapfer spät und früh, unverzagt in Stürmen
nspruchslose Infanterie Möge Gott dich schirme

28.   Forces Cinema: the sign reads: 'Island Cinema' (1942).

. The *Soldatenheim*, now
and Hall.

30.   Platte Saline: Small Arms Training (German wartime photograph).

31.   Longis Common: 'Russian' Cemetery (1945).

Franzoesische Staatsangehoerige

1	Goldin	Cheim	geb. 19.3.86.	gets.	7.12.43.
2	Perlstein	Robert	17.9.09.		29.12.63.
3	Becker	Seib	3.11.77.		30.12.43.
4	Worms	Lucien	6.9.86.		7.1.14.
5	Stresskoski	?	16.3.17.		8.2.44.
6	Gordesson	Wiefried	23.12.03.		26.2.44.
7	Lipmann	Henri	5.9.85.		2.3.44.
8	Kirschblatt	Schmuhl	12.1.97.		26.4.44.

[handwritten postscript]

32. Last page of *Sonderführer* Richter's list of dead. The hand-written postscript reads: 'Compiled on the spot by the undersigned personally on 11. 5. 45,
by order of the Fortress Commandant, Lt-Col Schwalm. Wilh Richter Sdfhr
(Z)'.

33. Longis Road: German Military Cemetery (1945).

34. Aerial view of Alderney in summer 1942: Only earthworks are visible. Helgoland Camp is just complete, Norderney and Borkum Camps are under construction and wo: on Sylt Camp has barely started. (*Crown copyright reserved.*)

35. A magnified aerial view also from 1942, showing St. Anne at the bottom and for Tourgis (left) and Grosnez (right) with Helgoland Camp (centre) in between. The fuel dump is clearly seen in the centre of the picture and the Giffoine AA guns on the extreme left. (*Crown copyright reserved.*)

Treatment of these was not noticeably better than on the construction sites. The commander of the Harbour Guard in late 1942 was recorded by one leading seaman in his unit as repeatedly giving the instruction: 'Just kick them in the arse when they come. They are not human beings but animals'. And side by side with brutality there was again compassion. A German crane-driver at the harbour noted:

> 'Once, on 6 January [1943], whilst we were loading heavy wooden boards, a Russian was hit by a hook that slipped during the operation and he fell into the ship, roughly 6 metres down... I lowered two more Russians on a platform into the hold of the ship and lifted the victim with the crane. I told [the OT *Truppführer* present] to call an ambulance at once. He went away but no ambulance turned up. Then a truck arrived for an officer, whom I asked to remove the wounded man to a hospital. But even when I threatened to stop the loading he would not remove the man. After 30 minutes I got two Russians to drive the wounded man back to his camp. Two days later, on enquiry, I was told that the man had died.'

Another German working at the harbour as a stevedore for the firm of Blume was moved to pity by the condition of the Russians who worked beside him. They were, it is true, privileged in that they were receiving 15 *Reichsmarks* a month, that is about two pounds ten shillings at the rate of exchange obtaining; but they could not buy food with it. The stevedore commented:

> 'Every eight days or so, a boat went to the Casquets with food and it used to bring back the stale bread they had not eaten there. I used to take this bread and divide it up among the Russians.'

Fishing

One or two fishing boats manned by Guernseymen were allowed by the Germans to fish from Braye harbour on certain conditions. There were restrictions of time, because of off-shore firing practice, and of place, to discourage escape. The entire catch had to be handed over to FK 515 for disposal. The Germans attempted to put a marine infantryman on board each boat, but this was successfully resisted on the grounds that it made the fishermen military targets and legitimate objects for air attack by the Royal Air Force.

Fishing permits were issued for a specified period — for example, two months — and were typed in both German and English. The rather picturesque latter version is given below:

> '*Hafenkommandant* Alderney   [date]
>   *Permit for Fishing during the month(s) of...*
>   The fisherman [name] is hereby authorised with the permission

of the harbour commander to fish till a distance off two miles of the northern coast of the isle of Alderney. The rules concerning the limits of allowed territory and fishing at foggy weather are handed to him today. Fishing is forbidden on Thursdays (whole day) and Fridays up to 13 pm. This paper authorises for entering the port. This permit is also valuable for [name of assistant].

(Signed) The harbour commander.'

The 'rules concerning the limits of allowed territory' etc were also typed in German and English. The latter reads:

'Fishing is allowed from 8 am in a distance of 2 miles from the north side of the Island. At the fixed hour the fishermen has to present himself in the *Hafenkommandantur* in order to receive a paper of identity authorising him to enter the harbour. This paper is given back after his return from fishing.
It is strictly forbidden:-

(1)   to land on the islands in the north of Alderney and to go fishing behind them, so that fishing boats must always remain visible.
(2)   to go out fishing in foggy or moist weather. If weather turns bad after having begun fishing, immediate return is necessary.
(3)   the selling of fish to any private or military person. All fish are at the disposal of the *Feldkommandantur*. It will be payed for by the *Feldkommandantur*.

The orders of any patrol-boat are in any case strictly to be obeyed. The consequence of not observing the reglementations will be defense of fishing, requisition of the boat and punishment by military laws.
Boats must return to harbour not later than one hour before sunset.

(signed) Commander of the Port.'

Wrecks

Reference has already been made to the 'Xaver Dorsch' (ex-'Staffa') which was blown off its mooring in January 1943 with a cargo of forced labourers on board. She went aground on the rocks at the south-west base of the stone jetty.

A derelict dredger lay in the south-west corner of the New Harbour.

The barge 'Marguerite' lay wrecked on Braye Beach just inside the Old Harbour wall.

Another wreck lay on the rocks in the middle of Braye Bay. It had been one of the harbour guard vessels that had come adrift in a storm in winter 1943 and been driven across the bay by the gale. In early

1944, the Germans considered the possibility of raising it for repair, but the plan was abandoned as too difficult.

Lost RAF crew

Some time between the Allied landing in Normandy (6 June 1944) and the fall of Cherbourg (end of June), an RAF bomber, described by the AA gunners on Alderney as a Lancaster, was shot down over the Race south-south-west of Essex Castle. Observers do not agree as to whether four or five survivors baled out and landed by parachute on the sea. Their descent was reported, but the Harbour Commandant refused to authorise rescue sortie by one of the harbour guard vessels. This surprised his staff, as one of his petty officers and one able seaman said in a joint statement:

> 'Although the weather was very fine, we were given no orders to put to sea in an attempt to rescue the airmen who were in danger of drowning. All of us were surprised that nothing was done for their rescue, whilst on other occasions we were ordered out by the Harbour Commandant, *Korvettenkapitän* Massmann, even if it was only to recover a drifting wooden crate.'

CHAPTER EIGHT

Quality of Life

SOME ASPECTS of the quality of life — or lack of it — in Alderney during the occupation years have already been discussed, even at length. It depended a bit on who you happened to be. At one end of the spectrum, a political prisoner in Sylt Camp or a forced labourer at Helgoland or Norderney was concerned only with survival in the face of under-nourishment, ill-treatment, overwork and exposure, in an environment where both man and nature can have seemed to offer him little but hostility in his extremity. Prisoners of war were more fortunate, and on a sliding scale with Russians at the bottom, Italians in the middle and Moroccans, oddly enough, at the top of the league; the latter were in the privileged position of receiving Red Cross parcels containing cigarettes which they traded to the Germans for favours of one kind or another. Next came the small number of civilian employees, who led relatively free lives, earned and spent money, had access to some canteen facilities and were more or less adequately fed, housed and clothed. Finally, the Armed Forces and their para-military ancillaries, the Germans in occupation.

There are always relative exceptions to any generalisation. There will, no doubt, have been moments when a German soldier derived great satisfaction from the vegetables he had grown in his billet garden, or when Major Hoffmann felt justifiably proud of brilliant use of ground in siting a machine gun nest. And of course it was indisputable that the Russian front was always an alternative which offered both greater hardship and shorter expectation of life. But in spite of all that, almost to a man the Germans in Alderney were unhappy, hated their time on the Island and regarded it as an undeserved, penitential experience. One even ran into verse about how dreadful life was *'auf Alderney, auf Alderney'*.

'Social welfare'

Soldiers of all armies are familiar with the boredom of garrison life, and their commanders are at pains to keep them as busy on duty, and as diverted off it, as they are able to make provision. In a remote and isolated garrison this would inevitably pose problems; without a civilian population living its life around them those problems could only be greater. Worst of all was the lack of female company.

The German Armed Forces in their wisdom normally made provision for the sexual distraction of their troops in occupied territory by running or making use of brothels under official supervision. In France, for example, most urban garrisons were able to avail themselves of an efficient network of houses of pleasure maintained under the watchful eye of the German military government and subject to regular inspection by civilian doctors or German medical officers. Admission to the better establishments was by appointment and card; in addition to which there was ample provision on a smaller, less formalised scale. Even in Jersey and Guernsey the Germans established such houses for their troops — in the latter case creating some friction over which was the competent authority to provide the ladies' rations and whether or not they should be classed as heavy workers.

But in Alderney life was rugged by comparison. A small number of women who had been brought over from France served as prostitutes, but this was neither regularly organised nor on the scale to which a garrison of 3,000 men might in happier circumstances have felt entitled. The OT staff ran its own separate establishment in a house in the centre of St Anne.

Private enterprise also played its part. Several of the officers ran independent households with the French lady of their choice. Lieutenant-Colonel Zuske lived in Connaught Square with a Frenchwoman of Polish extraction named Marianne, said to be from Evreux. One of his staff-officers was similarly installed with a Frenchwoman named Paulette, whom Zuske took on a tour of the Island's fortifications. This was popularly believed to have been the cause of Zuske's posting in 1943. Rumour said he had been sent to the Russian front, but in fact fate and his Adjutant-General seem to have been less unkind and he was moved to a desk job in the headquarters of the military district (*Wehrbezirkskommando*) in Leipzig, his home town. *Polizeiinspektor* Sturm, the guardian of law and order, lived with a Frenchwoman who became pregnant and went home to St Malo, to return at a later date with her figure restored. Major Hoffmann ran quite a lively establishment in one of the more discreetly isolated houses at the east end of the Island, near the fire control tower; both the murals and some of the finds in the garden when the Island was re-occupied suggest that he was not selfish in his pursuit of those joys.

Private enterprise was not only in terms of German military demand; there was also an element of female civilian supply. Some of the women brought in as civilian employees in canteens, kitchens, etc found a profitable use for their spare time in the transport lines of the NSKK below Essex Castle; others pursued their opportunities nearer home in the billets of St Anne. In the winter of 1942, some forty female workers were repatriated because they had contracted venereal disease and were spreading it among the troops. When Lieutenant-Colonel

Schwalm took over as Island Commandant at the end of 1943, he ordered the return of all female civilian employees to the other islands or to France, but about half a dozen managed to dodge the draft and remained in Alderney until the end of the war.

Canteens

The more general welfare of the troops was centred on the *Soldatenheim* — the nearest British equivalent would be NAAFI — a rest and recreation centre with a small canteen; it also offered certain limited shopping facilities, for example, artificial honey and artificial coffee, extra bread and sometimes French beer. The *Soldatenheim* was located off Connaught Square in one of the more prestigious buildings on the Island, once the home of the hereditary governor, in pre-war and immediate post-war years a Roman Catholic convent and school, and today the Island Hall — what contemporary urban Britain would no doubt call the civic centre. It was open to all members of the Armed Forces, with a reserved room for officers. German members of ancillary or para-military organisations were also admitted. The garden was cultivated to produce extra vegetables for the canteen. The whole establishment was run under the administration of the *Feldkommandantur* with the help of civilian employees, prisoners and forced labourers.

German troops were allowed to purchase some extra food from their unit canteen. They were issued with a ration of three cigarettes per day and could buy tinned milk and brandy. This led to a lively cross trade of black market rates between the troops, who needed more cigarettes, and the Moroccan prisoners of war who received ten packets of 20 each in their monthly Red Cross parcels; also in the opposite direction between the troops who could buy milk and brandy cheap and sell it at a substantial profit (buy at RM 6.50, sell at RM 45 was one rate quoted) to the paid civilian employees who had much restricted rights of canteen purchase.

The canteen for civilian employees was described by one of them:

> '[It was] in a dress shop at the corner of Victoria Street and High Street.... This was run by French girls under the direction of a German officer. The standard price for most articles seemed to be one mark. For this one could buy at the canteen (any of) the following:
>
> > 5 lighter flints
> > 2 thimblefuls of Calvados
> > 3-inch bar of cream filled chocolate (very scarce)
> > 5 small Petit Beurre biscuits
> > 6 Fruit Drops
> > 1 pair leather boot laces
> > 1 tin of black boot polish.'

At the imposed rate of exchange the civilians found this very expensive. There was no legal way for a civilian to obtain cigarettes or alcohol in excess of the thimblefuls quoted above.

Apart from these welfare centres, some units had canteen and rest huts of their own. This was less necessary and more modest in the case of the Engineer Staff's canteen in St Anne, but large and more isolated units like the *Westbatterie* and the Flak at Mannez had quite substantial accommodation for this purpose in heated wooden huts, well decorated with murals reminiscent of home.

Other facilities

Communications with the outside world were poor. The troops received and dispatched their mail through the Field Post Office (*Feldpostamt*), half way along Braye Street. But mails were dependent upon shipping, and shipping, as we have seen, was erratic. Moreover, ships sometimes arrived without mail, for which the troops blamed administrative inefficiency even when this was not the case. On one occasion this led to such heated official complaint by the garrison that disciplinary measures were threatened.

In theory newspapers were available. The German Armed Forces published a military newspaper in Paris, which got delivered by the Cherbourg convoys, and a military newspaper for the Channel Islands ('*Die Inselzeitung*') was also printed in Jersey and found its way to Alderney somewhat spasmodically.

Civilian employees from the other islands were less fortunate. They recorded delays of between six and eight weeks in mail delivery and had no newspapers except those sent by post from friends or relatives, subject to similar delay.

A Forces Book Shop (*Frontbuchhandlung*) was located in Victoria Street, where the troops could obtain reading matter, and the *Soldatenheim* was encouraged to keep a stock of suitable material for those relaxing there. Guide books were painstakingly translated into German and republished — with their original peacetime photographs — and standard tourist maps of the islands were reprinted with German legends for the benefit of the garrisons. A member of a National Socialist Propaganda Company (*Nationalsozialistische Propaganda-kompagnie* — NSPK), a sort of war correspondent, made a film of life in Alderney. The National Socialist Party maintained right to the end a full time officer (*Nationalsozialistischer Führungsoffizier* —NSFO) to stock and disseminate party literature; the legacy of books and pamphlets he left at the time of the surrender in May 1945 filled several rooms in a large house.

There were, of course, no private wireless sets permitted. But communal sets were available and in use at the *Soldatenheim* and in canteens, etc.

A Forces Cinema operated on the site of the pre-war Rink Cinema (later Lyceum, now demolished). Civilian employees were admitted on Tuesdays and Thursdays.

Every six weeks or so, a Roman Catholic chaplain visited the Island from Cherbourg and stayed two to three days.

Currency

The German Armed Forces were for most of the war paid in German notes (*Reichskreditkassenscheine*) and coin. Civilian employees were paid or credited in English currency at the exchange rate of 1 *Reichsmark* = 2/1½d. Forced labourers, as we have seen, had a sum in German currency credited in bulk to the employing firms but seldom actually received any pay. Prisoners, of course, were not paid at all.

In 1944-45 the troops were paid in French francs and German money was exchanged at the rate of 1 *Reichsmark* = 20 francs.

Inconveniences

Of all the unlikely things to loom large in the catalogue of woes for a garrison that felt it had so much cause to be sorry for itself, perhaps vermin comes as a surprise. Not personal vermin, the lice of the Russian front; but rats and rabbits. The cessation of widespread competent farming led to a multiplication of rabbits which interfered with the Germans' agricultural operations and the vegetable plots of the garden growers. The absence of normal standards of living and cleanliness of a civilian population, and above all, perhaps of house-proud wives, resulted not only in a massive increase in the rat population but also in their progressive migration into the inhabited areas. This was both a nuisance and a health hazard.

But epidemic, when it came, struck from another quarter. In 1942, the troops — and civilian employees — were attacked by an infection which caused diarrhoea, sometimes accompanied by a rash and worms under the skin. The clinical diagnosis of this at the time does not appear to have survived, but it has been suggested by one qualified to judge that the cause was probably a parasite, perhaps ascariasis, due to the insanitary conditions. Some of those affected believed their trouble was caused by milk from diseased cows, others blamed the water. It must be remembered that at peak Alderney was inhabited by more than three times its normal population, all of whom drank water and all of whom made sewage, so that it would not be surprising if existing facilities were overstretched for a time; indeed, it is recorded that in 1942 additional water supplies were pumped from York Hill Quarry into a concrete cistern between that quarry and the harbour, and that at least one emergency cargo of water was brought in by sea from France.

In addition to the inconveniences of nature, isolation and war, the garrison suffered from that constant bane of soldiers everywhere who lack active operations: repetitive practice drills. They dug holes and filled them in again. There were air-raid practices; although RAF raids were few and far between, the threat remained constant. There were stand-to alerts and anti-gas drills to keep the troops on their toes. The civilian employees, who had not been issued with gas-masks, found the latter a cause for speculative alarm as well as a nuisance.

CHAPTER NINE

The Dead

NOW THAT we have considered the occupation of Alderney over most of its course and across the spectrum of its various aspects, let us cast a retrospective look at those who died. We have to a large extent already seen how most of them died, and why, but there is yet another dimension discernible if we look at the picture as a whole. It must also be remembered that not only prisoners and forced labourers but also members of the German Armed Forces died in Alderney, and they are of interest both in their own right and as a comparative study. We shall then be in a position to analyse the data at the end of the chapter and to arrive at some conclusions on numbers.

But first, the work force: as with the rations, so with the death certificates; what happened in theory and on paper was not always what happened on the ground.

OT Procedure

When a forced labourer died, it was usually in camp; if not, then he was normally brought back to his camp. In some cases a corpse found outside was the subject of enquiry by the *Feldgendarmerie*, in which event a doctor was required to state formally that no post mortem examination was necessary before the body was released to the OT. At this point a death certificate (*Totenschein*) was issued. The certificate was usually signed by the camp sick-bay staff — for example, in Norderney Camp by Dr Dalgat, the Russian émigré doctor from France who was himself an inmate and not a German official. A copy of each certificate was kept at the camp and two copies were sent by the OT Camp Commander's staff to the OT *Frontführung* at the Alderney *Bauleitung*. The member of the *Bauleitung* staff responsible for welfare then addressed an executive report (*Vollzugsmeldung*) to the OT *Frontführung* at the OT *Oberbauleitung* at Cherbourg (or St Malo) with a copy to their welfare or personnel department officer and further copies to the Out-Station of FK 515, one for onward transmission to the Island Commandant. This executive report informed addressees of the date and cause of death and gave personal particulars of the deceased.

In the early days — mid-1942 — the procedure was not too strict and higher authority was not usually informed of the cause of death, but by autumn it was always included in the executive report from the

Alderney *Frontführung*. From late 1942 onwards, this executive report took on a standard form, an actual specimen of which reads as follows:

'Org Todt   On Active Service
Operations Group West   (date)
Sector Alderney   (reference)
Field Post No 19500
Welfare Office

Executive Report

Subject: Death of the Russian worker Eugen Saikowski
        born: 31.6.26 at Gluchow

On the 17.11.42 the Russian worker Eugen Saikowski of the firm Wolfer & Goebel in Operation Adolf, Field Post No 19500, died of dysentery.

The deceased was driven by truck from Norderney Camp to the town churchyard and thence carried by his comrades to his grave. A cross is being prepared by the firm for erection on the grave.

Personal Particulars: Name: Saikowski
                              First Name: Eugen
                              Born: 31.6.26
                              Marital status: unknown
                              Trade: unskilled labourer
                              Nationality: Ukrainian
                              Employer: Wolfer & Goebel
                              Died: 17.11.42
                              Buried: 18.11.42

Distribution

Frontführung, St Malo   (Signed)
Personnel Section, St Malo   Welfare Officer
FK 515 Adolf (2)
Sector Adolf Construction Office — Welfare
Department.'

This text illustrates both the practice of loosely calling Poles and Ukrainians as well as Russians 'Russian', and the use of the codename 'Adolf' for Alderney. (Since Alderney is mentioned in clear in the same text, the security value of the codename is questionable.)

After certification, the body was buried. The firm of Kniffler was charged with the task of burial. It supplied the gravedigger — a grotesque figure with one eye and reputedly not quite right in the head — and a coffin with a collapsible false bottom from which each corpse, or even a batch of two or three, could be deposited while the coffin remained to hand for the next customer. The hearse was a truck provided by the NSKK on demand from the OT.

On occasion, particularly at the beginning, forced labourers were buried in the parish churchyard. Most such burials were adjoining the north side of the church, where the car park now is, but a few were at the south end near New Street. The overwhelming majority were taken to a plot of waste ground on Longis Common, surrounded by a simple barbed wire fence, which became known as the 'Russian' Cemetery. The sandy soil there was very easy to dig. Most were buried in parallel rows at the north-eastern end of this cemetery, and eventually were marked with crosses bearing 'Russian' names. On the north-western side was one row of eight Jewish graves. On the south-western side were a number of unmarked graves.

OT Practice

Of course, what actually happened was not always just like that.

It may strike one as casual that the death certificates were not authenticated by a medical officer with official status; the inmate of a forced labour camp, be he never so well qualified a medical practitioner, has no authority; and an OT *Frontführung* Welfare Officer has no medical qualification. But this attitude did not stop there. Even after September 1942, when the standard executive report always included a cause of death, the way in which certification was carried out does not inspire confidence. Some death certificates did not give a cause of death, some were not signed and some had both omissions. For example, the executive report in respect of Eugen Saikowski quoted above specified that he died of dysentery; his death certificate from the camp sick-bay has a blank space against 'Cause of Death' and is unsigned. In the case of Philip Nowak, an Ukrainian who died on 17 November 1942 aged 21, his death certificate specified 'heartfailure from debility' (*Herzschwäche durch Entkräftung*) but the executive report gave his cause of death as tuberculosis. And Antoni Onuchowski, the circumstances of whose violent death were described in Chapter Three, was certified as having died of poisoning.

As *Verwaltungsoberinspektor* Hans Spann, who took over the Out-Station of FK 515 on Alderney in April 1942, commented:

> 'When a foreign worker died, the OT *Frontführung* sent me a copy of the death certificate ... It was already my opinion at that time that not too much reliability could be attached to such a certificate.'

The erection of crosses in the cemetery was no more reliable. It was supposed to be a part of Kniffler's burial responsibilities, delegated to the one-eyed gravedigger. But in practice? Again Spann commented:

> 'On one of my tours of the fields I had the opportunity to visit the OT (Russian) cemetery. I was struck by the disorder and marked lack of dignity with which the corpses had been buried; moreover

I had the impression that on some occasions more than one body had been put in one grave. Because the graves were not marked, I made a report ... pointing out the repulsive conditions which I had found at the cemetery ... Following my complaint the unmarked graves were given names; but I am extremely doubtful if the names on the individual graves were correct.'

An analysis of the names on the graves gives some support to Spann's scepticism. Captain Kent, Staff Officer 3 (Public Safety) in 20 Civil Affairs Unit, Alderney, made a survey of the graves dated 7 June 1945. He drew attention to the fact that nine crosses in Row 7 at the 'Russian' cemetery bore a second name either underneath the name of the initial body or on the reverse side; one of these was that same Eugen Saikowski whose death certificate was so uninformative. Nearby was part of a tenth cross with a new name but not on a grave. Moreover, it appeared that nine names appeared on crosses both in the 'Russian' cemetery and in the parish churchyard with the same names and dates. *Frontführer* Johann Hoffmann made a gallant attempt to explain the first phenomenon:

'The gravedigger did get the order to inscribe the crosses anew when they became illegible. He took them to his workshop and re-erected them later in the wrong places. That is why the chronological sequence is incorrect in some rows.'

But neither Hoffmann nor *Sonderführer* Wilhelm Richter, who replaced Spann, could explain the duplication of names on different graves. Richter stated on 4 June 1945:

'*Major* Kratzer, the *Feldkommandant* in Guernsey [i.e. Richter's immediate superior] told me in Guernsey that when I arrived here [March 1944] I was to see that the graves in the Russian cemetery had crosses on them. I went to the cemetery and found the last seven graves had no crosses. I saw a heap of crosses there, nearly all had names on them. I used them for the last seven graves. All the other graves had crosses. I do not know in which grave the people whose name appeared on the crosses were buried. I asked that question myself and was told that they had new crosses put on their graves.

I cannot explain where the people are buried whose names appear on the reverse side of eight of the crosses in the ['Russian'] cemetery. I cannot understand why the graves have crosses which are not in chronological order of death. I can give no explanation as to why Fernand Jardin [actually Lardin] appears to be buried twice in St Anne's churchyard... There are no lists now.'

In fact there were still two lists. Indeed Richter himself had drawn them up the previous month, but they were based on the garbled detail of the crosses and therefore inaccurate; for which, perhaps, at that late stage, Richter is hardly to blame. Any subsequent list has been based on the same faulty data, but it is the best we now have available.

The concentration camp

The SS procedure in the concentration camp, as is to be expected, differed from that of the OT and its forced labourers. The SS were not accountable outside their own service, and the question of certificates or executive reports being copied to the Island Commandant or FK 515 did not arise. Nevertheless, as in establishments administered by the SS *Totenkopfverband* elsewhere, great store was set by the semblance of legality, and so death certificates there had to be.

The care of the sick in Sylt Camp was in the hands of doctors who happened to be among the prisoners. As such, of course, their signatures were not valid on official documents. So *Hauptsturmführer* List and his successor Braun both insisted that, in the absence of a resident SS medical officer, the death certificates prepared by the prison doctors should be signed by a medical officer of the Armed Forces, normally the senior medical officer, known as the Island Doctor (*Inselarzt*), later Fortress Doctor (*Festungsarzt*). This was at first *Oberarzt* (Lieutenant) Dr Uhl and later *Stabsarzt* (Captain) Dr Hans J. Hodeige. The signatory Armed Forces medical officer did not have direct knowledge of the circumstances attending a death in the concentration camp and was dependent upon the certificate put in front of him by the SS on the 'authority' of a doctor prisoner who was under total SS control. And the Armed Forces medical officer was not allowed to see the dead body he was called upon to certify.

The Army medical corps NCO who acted as clerk for the Fortress Doctor in 1944 said:

> 'The death certificates of Sylt Camp consisted of a printed form on which the cause of death, which was always heart failure or faulty circulation, was typed in. The cause of death was filled in by the SS. The death certificate was then presented to the Fortress Doctor for signature.'

'Heart failure' is a catch-all phrase of such indisputable accuracy that it must have appealed to the most logical, purist mind.

Nevertheless, not all medical officers in the Armed Forces were content with the honesty of this arrangement. An Air Force doctor on the HQ staff in Guernsey was consulted about it by his colleague with the Flak HQ in Alderney, *Stabsarzt* Dr Köhler:

> 'According to the information I received from my colleague Dr Köhler, *Stabsarzt* Dr Hodeige (at that time the Island Doctor) repeatedly signed death certificates for the Sylt concentration

camp on Alderney. These death certificates were printed in all details and even had the cause of death, heart failure, entered on the form. On one day four to six of these certificates were put before Dr Hodeige for signature. He signed these certificates without examining the bodies, without being given the opportunity to ascertain the cause of death... One day Dr Köhler rang me up to say that two printed death certificates from Sylt concentration camp had been presented to him for signature, with the cause of death already filled in as "heart failure"... He declared he would have nothing to do with the affair and passed it on to the naval medical officer, Dr Scherf.'

Within a year, very shortly before the end of the war, Dr Köhler committed suicide while the balance of his mind was disturbed.

A Spaniard who worked as a mechanic for the NSKK on Alderney recorded an incident which again illustrates both the unaccountability of the concentration camp administration and its outward conformity, this time with normal OT burial procedure:

'Among other fellow-workers I had three prisoners from the SS camp with me — two Germans and one Pole. The name of one of the Germans was Balder. Under orders from the NSKK NCO in charge, I had to take these three prisoners back to Sylt Camp by truck every evening between 7.30 and 8 pm.

During the month of August 1943, whilst arriving at Sylt as I have described, I saw the following. All the prisoners were lined up in the compound. In front of the parade two prisoners were kneeling with their hands clasped behind their necks. I found this unusual, but could not stay to observe further proceedings, as I was not allowed to wait longer than was necessary to unload my prisoners at the camp.

The following day I asked Balder about the incident and he told me that the two prisoners who had been kneeling in front of the parade had been condemned to death and were hanged the same evening in the presence of the prisoners.

In order to confirm whether this was really true, I asked a Spanish friend about it who was also employed by the NSKK... His special job was to transport corpses to the cemetery by truck. I asked him whether the two had really been hanged. He replied that when he went to collect those two corpses to take them to the cemetery, they still had part of the rope with which they had been hanged about their necks.'

Although the graves in the 'Russian' cemetery are apparently not in strict chronological sequence, there is a general tendency (according to their crosses) for early burials to have been in Rows 1-4 and later burials in Row 5 and upwards. As has been noted, the build up of OT labour preceded the arrival of the concentration camp, there was a period in 1943 when both were at peak, and then the OT phased out before the concentration camp. One would therefore expect a higher proportion of forced labourers' bodies in the early rows and of prisoners' bodies in the later rows. Johann Hoffmann said he thought all the latter were in Rows 5-7. There are some Germanic names among the 'Russians' in those rows to support this; moreover, no other place of burial has been mentioned by witnesses or documents.

The only date in August 1943 which has two burials listed on the same day is 27 August. Kent gives the names from the crosses in the 'Russian' cemetery as:

> Pedor Stastchuk, born 25.6.25, died 27.8.43 —No 7 in Row 5;
> and   Wladimir Kotupolenko, born 2.?.24, died 27.8.43 — No 33 in Row 5
> (who, according to Richter was: Upemladimir Kotol, born 12.2.24, died 17.8.43 — No 33 in Row 5).

Richter lists them as:

> Fedor Stastchak, born 25.6.25, died 27.8.43 —No 7 inRow 5;
> and   Iwan Ifewiska, born 1.3.19, died 27.8.43 — No 8 in Row 5
> (who, according to Kent was: Iwan Jewestignewjew, born 1.5.19, died 17.?.43 — No 8 in Row 5).

Can it be that Fyodor Stastchuk and either his neighbour in the cemetery, Ivan Yevestigneyev, or No 33 in the same row, Vladimir Kotopolenko, were the two men from Sylt Camp whose death was recorded by the Spaniard?

Numbers

Of course we must make due allowance for inaccuracies caused by the German (and our own) variations of orthography when spelling Slavonic names or transliterating them from Cyrillic script. But the German records in Alderney were so confusing that one cannot but doubt whether those traditionally so renowned for meticulous and efficient administration were in this instance really aiming at clarity. There are the death certificates, sometimes manifestly misleading; there are the executive reports, which do not always tally with the certificates; there are the names on the crosses, out of chronological sequence, in nine cases bearing two different names on the same grave with one body, and in 22 cases marking two graves in different places with the same names and dates of birth; there was Richter's list, in all its inaccuracy. All this we have already seen. But there was more.

Some were reported dead but have no known grave marked with their name. Two of the Russians who were still alive and in the Channel Islands in May 1945, one from Helgoland Camp and one from Norderney Camp, mentioned four friends from their home village who had died in autumn 1942; only one of these, Vassily Gorbatch, has a named grave and figures on a list. Gregori Pashko, aged 40, and Nikolai Vassilko, aged 23, are firmly stated by these two witnesses to have died in their beds in their hut in Helgoland Camp. One of them elaborated:

'When I saw Pashko and Vassilko after their death, their bodies were completely wasted away, so that they looked like skeletons. They had both asked for medical treatment, but neither had received it. After death, their bodies were dispatched to Norderney sick-bay and thence sent to burial. I am quite sure that they were dead because when I saw them in the morning, before they were taken to the sick-bay, rigor mortis had already set in.'

The same witnesses say Mikhail Bojko, aged 22, was taken to the sick-bay at Norderney Camp where he died at about the same time. Similarly, other surviving forced labourers have identified Vassíli Dolgov, a Russian aged 18, who was taken dying from Helgoland to Norderney, where he died in the sick-bay on 7 November 1942; and Stanislaw Schiller, a Pole born in 1923, who died in Helgoland Camp in the spring of 1943. Where are these buried ? None is named or listed. The unnamed graves may be the answer. And where is Fyodor Pachomov, born 5.3.04 at Sòsnivka, died 20.12.42, whose half-cross was found lying in the 'Russian' cemetery? And where is the prisoner Ebert whose death was considered in Chapter Five, but who figures on no list in any name remotely resembling that reported. And where are the Czech Josef Lammel and the German political prisoner, Rudi Busch, both shot by guards in the concentration camp?

Given these imponderables, it has indeed been difficult to view with confidence any firm statement of numbers. The most authoritative figure dates from the exhumation in 1963, which properly belongs to the next chapter, but it may be convenient to quote the figures here. When dug up, it was found there were more rows than Captain Kent had listed, some of them were found to contain different numbers of graves from those listed by Kent (and counted by the author) in 1945, and the number of bodies did not always correspond with the number of graves, viz:

Row	Graves	Bodies
1	35	35
2	35	35
3	36	36

4	37	37
5	38	38
6	38	39
7	37	41

There was in addition a further row at the north-eastern end:

| 8 | 29 | 29 |

And the two further burial areas on the western side contained respectively:

| (9) | 5 | 5 |
| (10) | 31 | 31 |

This gives a total of 326. It will originally have been 329, because the bodies of three French Jews had already been repatriated from the north-western corner in 1949.

In the parish churchyard, in 1945 there were 58 visible graves near the north wall of the church and five at the south end of the cemetery, all marked with crosses. The Commonwealth Graves Commission in 1960 listed 64 foreign workers buried there, broken down by nationalities as follows:

Belgian	1
Dutch	5
French	2
Polish	1
Russian	45
Spanish	1
Yugoslav	6
Unidentified	3

One of the unidentified is listed in other papers as a Czechoslovak citizen. The listed Pole is not Onuchowski, who has been included among the 45 'Russians'; but we have already commented on the use of the word 'Russian' to mean anything east of Germany.

On reburial, two of the named 'Russian' graves and two unidentified graves were found to contain no body, leaving a total of sixty.

Perhaps Johann Hoffmann should be given the last word on this particular theme:

> 'People who do not care for the lives of Russians will not bother much about their graves.'

The German Military Cemetery

The Germans had a military cemetery just north of the Longis Road at its junction with Valongis, behind the Strangers' Cemetery.

It was opened with the first member of the Armed Forces to die in Alderney on 4 February 1942, a lance-corporal named Link. It closed with another lance-corporal who died on 18 May 1945. It was reserved for members of the Armed Forces and the para-military and ancillary services. Thus, although the majority buried there were soldiers, sailors or airmen, also included were some minor anomalies like four volunteer workers and a Georgian legionary from the Caucasus. *Oberzahlmeister* Frank, whose suicide was recorded in Chapter Three, is one of the only two officers.

The cemetery was well and tidily kept and laid out in four rows of 14, 14, 15 and 18 graves respectively. Eleven of the graves in Row 4 were close together and contained the bodies of members of the Armed Forces killed in a naval engagement off Cherbourg in June 1944. Two of the early graves also belong to corpses washed up on the Island, one a German naval rating, the other unidentified.

The cemetery also contained the bodies of the only two fatal casualties in Alderney when HMS 'Rodney' shelled the *Batterie Blücher* on 12 August 1944 and severely damaged No. 3 gun.

Up to March 1945, when it must have been impossible to visit the Island, all crosses bore a little metal disc with the lettering 'WGO 13' and a number. The latter was the serial number under which the grave was registered by the Armed Forces Graves Officer No 13 (*Wehrmachtsgräberoffizier* = WGO).

Richter adds an interesting postscript to his list, not recorded elsewhere. He names seven suicides among the German garrison on Alderney — one in 1942, five in 1943 and one in 1944 — and two executions by firing squad after court-martial, both in April 1945. All of these were, he wrote, buried in the parish churchyard.

He also noted the burial there of Private Leonard J. Cross, of 'A' Company, 35 Regiment (?), US Army, whose body had been washed ashore on 14 January 1945.

Comparative Analysis

We are now in a position to consider the significance of the statistics in relation to the deaths which took place in Alderney during the occupation. We may not with confidence be too mathematically precise, and of course there is no means now of knowing how many more went into the sea like the mussel-eaters of Chapter Three or who may have died after leaving the Island, but as a result of events there. But certain minimum conclusions can safely be made.

The earliest recorded death among the forced labourers and prisoners was on 26 February 1942 and the latest on 22 June 1944. Between those dates at least 389 died, 329 buried in the 'Russian' cemetery and 60 in the parish churchyard. This was out of a work force which in its peak period, though not throughout, will have totalled over 3,000. On the basis of the figures available, their average age at death was just over 26. Of them 44 were teen-agers (four only 16) and 16 were over 40 (one 61, one 51).

Over the same period of nearly 2½ years, 20 members of the

German Armed Forces died in Alderney, out of a garrison of over 3,000 for most of the time.

The worst months for the labour force were November and December 1942, during which about 100 died (97 according to Richter, 101 according to Kent, 116 according to the surviving executive reports. These latter, may, of course, not be complete and, as we have shown, are not wholly accurate; but if they err it will not be in exaggeration of the truth.). In other words 116 is probably a minimum. A breakdown of this figure shows that the victims were 58 Ukrainians, 42 Russians, 14 Poles, 1 Frenchman and 1 Dutchman, and gives their official causes of death as:

Dysentery	—	22
Cachexy	—	22
Dysentery and Cachexy	—	14
Poisoning	—	29
Tuberculosis	—	10
Exhaustion/heart failure	—	8
Other	—	11

In those two months no single death took place among the Armed Forces. Even when German military rations were cut to their lowest under blockade in 1945, the total deaths in the garrison from all causes were only 21 for the five months January to May inclusive.

So when the last Island Commandant, Lieutenant-Colonel Schwalm, blithely commented:

'The number of deaths [in the labour force] ... did not give rise to any suspicion with regard to either number or cause, as compared with the troops',

he may have been a little over-sanguine. Unease of conscience had already peeped through the cracks in normality as far as many of his command were concerned.

CHAPTER TEN

Aftermath

THE SURRENDER of the German Forces in Jersey and Guernsey took place on 9 May 1945. There had been some uncertainty over the willingness of the garrisons in the Channel Islands to give automatic effect to the capitulation to which the German Armed Forces as a whole had just submitted. This uncertainty remained after 9 May in respect of the most isolated garrison, in Alderney. So it was not until 16 May that the first British troops from Force 135 formally took re-possession of the Island.

Within the first few days well over two thousand of the garrison had been shipped out to prisoner of war camps and work had begun to remove the more significant hardware among the fortifications. A working party of about 500 Germans from the garrison, reinforced later by a few more from the other islands, got down to clearing up the sterile residue of war. In some cases, for example the open gun pits of the AA troop south-west of the Marette, a whole strong-point could be bull-dozed back into the field in half a day. The more elaborate concrete works have defied the demolition squad to this day. They were too many, contained too much concrete and were too prone to cause neighbouring damage to be readily blown up in situ, and any piecemeal removal was a labour indeed as was seen in the few cases where it was attempted. Most of the barbed wire (why not all, one asks oneself?) was removed by this small force of prisoners of war, who were based at Borkum Camp, now renamed Minerva Camp under new management. Ammunition stocks were dumped at sea. The mines were a problem for a time.

The German working parties lifted their own mines with commendable speed, at the rate of over 300 a day. And the German engineer officer in charge was prevailed upon to make spot checks on the ground cleared, as a guarantee that the work was well done. It was decided for reasons of safety to explode the mines in batches near the sites. The trouble was that the shock waves through the solid rock did damage elsewhere in the Island if the explosions were too great. The mines were, therefore, often lifted at a faster rate than they were destroyed, and for a time those abroad in outlying districts could suddenly find their way endangered by stacks of unexploded mines. But it was soon over.

For a few weeks more the last remains of the old work force lingered on awaiting repatriation. A handful of forced labourers had remained working on the Island right to the end, and in June a Soviet officer, Major V. Gruzdev, arrived to interview the Soviet citizens among them; he sought to see the Poles and others as well, but their enthusiasm did not match his own, perhaps because of unhappy circumstances elsewhere. The hard core of the ladies who had evaded Schwalm's more puritanical interpretation of the role of French female auxiliary labour had also not yet returned to France in June.

Very soon work started to prepare Alderney for the return of its population. The Germans had destroyed a number of houses completely, notably on Platte Saline, to improve the field of fire of their weapons. These had to be replaced and those less completely ruined made serviceable again. But the German legacy was not all negative. The water reservoir was extended and the supply system proved a good foundation on which the present arrangements were built; the concrete observation tower on the Mouriaux had an extra storey added on top and has since served as a water tower. Some new stretches of road had been laid to give access to German emplacements, but most important from the Island's point of view was the concrete surface, largely on top of the old road, from Whitegates via Braye and Crabby to the approach to Fort Tourgis. The electricity network was a big bonus and was readapted gradually to the different needs and locations of the civilian population; indeed the German wiring in the author's cottage was not replaced until 1976. The generating capacity had been due for extension in 1945, and six French generators still lay in their packing cases; these were duly returned to France. The extension to the harbour jetty was not such a useful asset in terms of Alderney's peace-time requirements; after some use in the immediate post-war days when traffic was heavy, its woodwork fell gently into decay and became unsafe; the metal structure was finally removed in 1978/79. And Odoire's, whose bakery had been taken over by the German Armed Forces in 1940, were able to take possession of the German military bakery on its new site.

Some unhappy marks of what had happened were still in evidence. Despite the destruction of Helgoland Camp, its stone entrance pillars still stood — and stand today, but now more happily integrated into the newly developed streetscape. The false-bottomed coffin was still lying in the rank grass of the 'Russian' cemetery which, despite half-hearted attempts to make it more presentable before the British saw it, offered a fair picture of desolation. The Commandant's châlet at Sylt Camp had not been destroyed in 1944 with the rest of the buildings; it was moved to Longis and used as a private dwelling — and has since had two wings added.

Its original occupant, *Hauptsturmführer* List, did not stay long in

Norway. He returned to Berlin, where he was promoted to the rank of SS *Sturmbahnführer* (Major) and was posted to Italy in June 1944. Immediate post-war records showed that List, like his SS henchmen Klebeck and Braun, had not survived. However, the Federal German Public Prosecutor's Office has recently been quoted as stating that Maximilian List of SS *Baubrigade* I gave evidence before a Hamburg court in 1974 (in a matter unconnected with Alderney).

It was the agreed policy of the victorious powers that war criminals should in principle be tried in the Allied country where the offence had taken place; apart from the legal conveniences, such as local witnesses, this was a natural retributive claim by heavily aggrieved nations like the Poles, the French or the Russians. In the case of Alderney a more or less unique situation existed: there were effectively no local witnesses and the victims were not nationals of the country where the offence had occurred. It was therefore decided in London that it would be wrong for Britain to attempt to represent her aggrieved Allies who should themselves try those in custody against whom serious charges could be preferred.

So copies of the Alderney investigation report were passed to the Russians along with the offer of Carl Hoffmann for trial; he was said to have been hanged at Kiev in the autumn of 1945. It has recently been suggested that he died in West Germany in the mid-1970s, but resolving this apparent discrepancy lies outside the scope of this wartime record. Karl Tietz's successor, OT *Haupttruppführer* Adam Adler, and his assistant, OT *Meister* Heinrich Evers, were less fortunate than Tietz had been; they were tried as war criminals by the French and sentenced to long periods of imprisonment. As these two have been the subject of some inaccuracy in the past, it may be worth noting here that although it is true that Adler was not only an OT *Haupttruppführer* but also an SS *Untersturmführer* (second lieutenant), he held this rank in the *Allgemeine* (General) SS, not in the *Totenkopfverband* which ran the concentration camps of the Third Reich. He was unconnected with Neuengamme, the parent unit of Alderney's concentration camp, and he did not hold a noteworthily low, and therefore senior, Party number, as has been suggested: it was, in fact, recorded as 330237. Evers does not appear to have been in the SS at all.

The disgraceful conditions at the town lock-up which had been used for short-term military detainees were still un-remedied. Captain Kent's description included lavatories 'literally filled to the top with human excrement'. Happily the Garrison Officer, who was responsible, had been left on the Island with the working party and was able to play his part in helping to restore a more wholesome atmosphere.

The 'Staffa'/'Xaver Dorsch' was broken up for scrap where she lay on the rocks at the corner of the harbour. The 'Dorothea Weber' joined the Royal Navy.

All the German casualties in the Military Cemetery were reburied in the German War Graves Commission's cemetery at Mont de Huisnes, in the neighbouring French *département* of Manche in 1961. The German War Graves Commission also accepted responsibility for the forced labourers and prisoners who had technically been employees of the OT, and these were taken to Mont de Huisnes at the same time. The bodies of five French Jews among them were quickly re-routed from Mont de Huisnes to a more acceptable resting place in the Cimetière de St Ouen at St. Denis, near Paris. The Memorial generously erected and maintained by the Hammond family is their only monument in Alderney today; appropriately enough it overlooks Longis Common. A plaque in the north wall of the parish church is the memorial to those buried in the churchyard.

In 1977, a family Bible which had been removed from Alderney for safe keeping by a German naval officer in 1941 was returned by him to the Island. His covering letter concluded: 'My prayer is that in your country and in mine peace may be kept'.

*   *   *

No doubt many great questions remain unsolved. Two of the smaller ones lie on the top of the author's pending tray:

Where did the aircraft engine come from, lodged all by itself in a cleft half way up the south cliffs, discovered in 1947 by the author and a friend climbing with the help of German army ladders (which are now no longer there)?

Who was Erika, immortalised in wet concrete on the parapet of a small bunker on the top of Essex Hill on 18 March 1943?

*   *   *

Alderney was not associated with happiness in the years of the occupation. The garrison was bored and frustrated. The labour force was hungry and brutally treated. The Islanders were in exile. But of course it can be argued, as the phrase had it at the time, there was a war on, and that covers the multitude of inconveniences and sufferings that war by its nature brings, often much worse than in Alderney's case.

But can one dismiss so lightly and automatically the gratuitous death of some hundreds of men, mainly young and in their prime? They did not die because the fortunes of war blew them up. They did not die in defence of something dear to them or elect to take a risk that turned out disastrous for them. They died because they were arbitrarily freighted to Alderney willy-nilly and starved and worked to death.

Some may find it all too easy to jump to the conclusion that all the Germans were equally to blame. Others may shirk the concept of blame or feel that it all happened a long time ago and is not any real business of theirs. If this book has a purpose, it is to make it as hard as possible to follow any of those easy options. There must be blame for those unnecessary deaths, but let it be based on informed judgement and some attempt, however imperfect, to be just. There were individual Germans on Alderney who may deserve that judgement, just as there were others who do not. And there will no doubt have been others too, in Cherbourg, in St. Malo, in Paris, and indeed in Berlin, who had a share of responsibility that they cannot escape.

Finally let us not forget those unfortunates in the worst case of all, who having survived one inhumanity may have returned home to another, not welcomed, their wounds not healed nor their life restored, but blamed by their rulers for working for the German enemy and consequently condemned as traitors.

* * *

In 1978, the poet John Moat paid a visit to Alderney. He wrote a poem which, with great sensitivity, captures both past suffering and the healing qualities of the Island. He has kindly allowed this book to end with his words:

ALDERNEY

On the Longy Road the ghosts freeze.
They have done their time;
With the gale the siren will cease.

A new sound is whetting the wind —
Out there on the Fort flows the clean wine
Death left behind.

In waves there is laughter, on the breeze
a clear song. The causeway shines,
We have raised the siege.

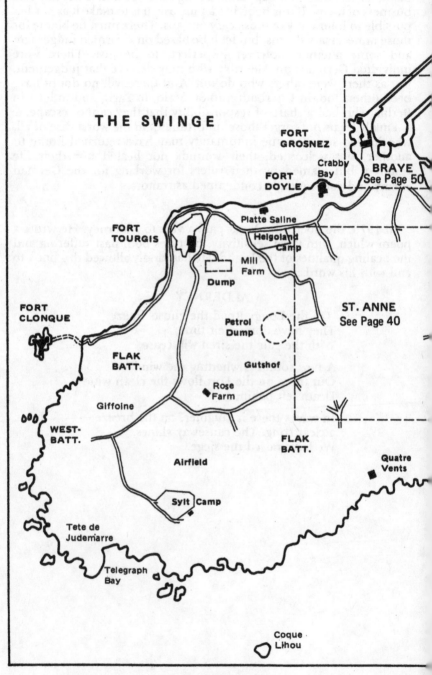

Map of Alderney, 1943/4

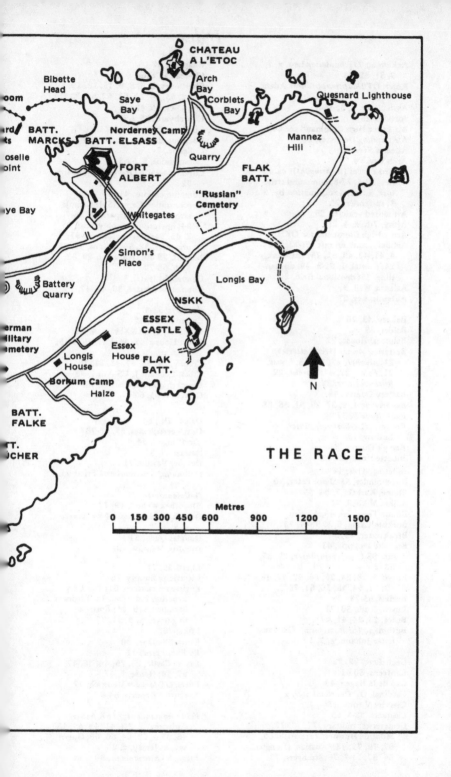

Index

ADDENDA AND CORRIGENDA

Page 2, 6 lines from bottom: *after* '... 1942 run from Cherbourg.' *add* 'This first occupation force included a dozen *Luftwaffe* signallers tasked with spotting British aircraft and reporting by radio. Initially there was no regular channel of supply and the little garrison lived on food stocks abandoned by the evacuated islanders.'

Page 5, 7 lines from bottom: *after* '... lent his name' *read* 'to one of the ships serving the Germans in Alderney; it was wrecked at Braye in 1943.'

Page 29, 3 lines from bottom: *below* 'Among these were:' *add*
    Hauptscharführer   –   Knop, from Orianienburg, in
    (Sergeant-Major)   charge of camp administration
                           June to November 1943

Page 29, last line: *after* Georg Gerk entry *add*
                           Puhr, a Sudeten German in charge
                           of administration early 1943

Page 30, 4 lines from bottom: *between* 'Rometsch' and 'Wolf' *add* 'Toschkewirt'

Page 35, line 10: *for* 'Ebert' *read* 'Willi Everts'

Page 35, lines 13, 19, 25 and 32: *for* 'Ebert' *read* 'Everts'

Page 36, line 2: *after* '... over the cliff.' *add* 'There were two multiple shootings accounting for nearly 50 prisoners in all; but despite German attempts to conceal the cause of death, it has been possible to identify the victims and the record is clear.'

Page 37, line 23: *after* '... destination Buchenwald.' *add* 'Over five hundred survivors were liberated in Austria on 5 April 1945. Sergeant-Major Högelow was taken prisoner, tried and imprisoned.'

Page 56, 10 lines from bottom, under *Wrecks*, first two paragraphs to read:

'One of the inter-island ships, the 'Staffa', went aground on the rocks at the south-west base of the stone jetty in 1941, where its remains were still visible in 1945.

Reference has already been made to the 'Xaver Dorsch' which was blown off its mooring in January 1943 with a cargo of forced labourers on board.'

Page 70, line 8: *after* '... witnesses or documents.' *add* 'Neuengamme records suggest less than one hundred of the concentration camp prisoners died in Alderney. Most of these have been identified in the list of those buried there.'

Page 71, line 26: *for* 'Ebert' *read* 'Everts'

Page 72, 12 lines from bottom: *after* '... a total of sixty.' *add* 'There is thus evidence for rather less than four hundred deaths among the workforce on the island, a figure supported by the numbers exhumed, by the testimony of both Germans and forced labourers in 1945 and by the documentary records which have come to light since. The figure of nearly seven hundred which has been bandied about in recent years, to say nothing of even more sensational estimates, has never been substantiated.'

Page 77, line 3: *for* 'showed' *read* 'suggested'

Page 77, lines 19-23: *to read* 'Copies of the Alderney investigation report were prepared for the Russians who might, it was thought, have proceeded against the Island Commander in the worst years, Carl Hoffmann; but in the event he was repatriated as a prisoner of war and died in Germany in 1974.'

Page 77, line 27: *for* '... long periods of imprisonment.' *read* 'ten and seven years respectively.'